CIVILITY, COMPASSION, AND COURAGE IN SCHOOLS TODAY

CIVILITY, COMPASSION, AND COURAGE IN SCHOOLS TODAY

Strategies for Implementing in K–12 Classrooms

Patricia Kohler-Evans
and Candice Dowd Barnes

ROWMAN & LITTLEFIELD
Lanham • Boulder • New York • London

Published by Rowman & Littlefield
A wholly owned subsidiary of The Rowman & Littlefield Publishing Group, Inc.
4501 Forbes Boulevard, Suite 200, Lanham, Maryland 20706
www.rowman.com

Unit A, Whitacre Mews, 26–34 Stannary Street, London SE11 4AB

Copyright © 2015 by Patricia Kohler-Evans and Candice Dowd Barnes

All rights reserved. No part of this book may be reproduced in any form or by any electronic or mechanical means, including information storage and retrieval systems, without written permission from the publisher, except by a reviewer who may quote passages in a review.

British Library Cataloguing in Publication Information Available

Library of Congress Cataloging-in-Publication Data Available

ISBN 978-1-4758-0975-6 (cloth : alk. paper)—ISBN 978-1-4758-0976-3 (pbk : alk. paper)—ISBN 978-1-4758-0977-0 (electronic)

∞™ The paper used in this publication meets the minimum requirements of American National Standard for Information Sciences—Permanence of Paper for Printed Library Materials, ANSI/NISO Z39.48-1992.

Printed in the United States of America

This book is dedicated to those who protect and those who need protection; those who love and those who need to be loved; those whose lives have been affected by a lack of civility, compassion, or courage; and those who treat others with respect, empathy, and dignity.

CONTENTS

Preface		ix
1	Creating a Climate	1
2	A Theoretical Framework: The Model of Influence	7
3	Current Research and Classroom Applications	13
4	Bringing Civility to Life	25
5	Bringing Compassion to Life	37
6	Bringing Courage to Life	47
7	Lesson Plans in Civility	59
8	Lesson Plans in Compassion	75
9	Lesson Plans in Courage	89
10	Advice for School Leaders	103
Appendix A: Lesson Plan Template		113
Appendix B: Resources for Developing a PowerPoint, Prezi, or Blog		117

PREFACE

In the words of our friend and colleague, Mark Cooper, professor of early childhood at the University of Central Arkansas, "Don't wait for a difference maker. Go out and make a difference." In our long-standing work with Mark, he has served as the gently chiding voice that continuously and consistently suggests K–12 education is not just comprised of the teaching of mathematics, language arts and the like. According to Cooper, all is for naught unless the curriculum is infused with purposeful attention to those characteristics that truly define us, characteristics such as caring, gratitude, and compassion. What can we say? Mark's gentle promptings have urged us into action. His voice is now a deeply ingrained element in our collective voice.

We, Candice and Patty, have shared a common journey for the last several years. Each of us comes from a family with tenacious roots in public education. Each of us is known for our devotion to the causes surrounding kids of all ages, especially those for whom the world in which we live is less than kind. We must speak up rather than sit on the sidelines to make an appreciable difference in the lives of others. We must carry the torch of insistence that our educational system include more than Common Core State Standards, more than state frameworks, and more than the content areas that typically define us as public educators.

Although our journey in many ways has been shared, we come from slightly different backgrounds. Candice, an assistant professor, has worked in early childhood education and higher education for a number of years. Many of the earlier years were spent in the classroom and in leadership and professional development roles. The last several years have been in higher education. Her teaching is fueled by a philosophy that education is a means that allows one to contribute to the world in a profound and personal way. She is a proponent of social emotional learning and disposition development of students from preschool to adult learners, and she often collaborates with colleagues to develop innovative curriculum and instructional strategies for all learners. Patty, an associate professor, served for many years as a special education teacher and for numerous additional years in special education administration. Most of those administrative years were spent as the director of the division of exceptional children for a sizable urban district. She continues her work in schools as an executive coach for public school administrators and by facilitating instructional models that promote inclusion of all students within the learning community. She also works with Candice, Mark, and others in the Mashburn Center for Learning, which promotes social emotional learning and other instructional practices for all learners.

Our roads to this beloved place in higher education have given us unique perspectives as we seek to assist young teachers as they prepare to teach every child who enters their classrooms with a passion that transcends most human understanding. Our heartfelt desire is that each candidate who leaves our program, will in turn be a staunch advocate for the least as well as for the privileged. It is our collective belief that we are only successful in our work as those who leave our program stand armed with the skills and deep commitment to pay as much attention to the social emotional learning needs of their students as they do to the academic achievement of these same students. Only then will we have achieved our mission.

Through our daily conversations as friends and colleagues, the seeds for this book were planted. We wanted to share our collective insight to suggest, in tangible and concrete ways that yes, the characteristics of civility, compassion, and even courage, can be woven into the daily framework of our lessons. We can be purposeful, and we can make tremendous differences in the lives of our K–12 students.

During the writing of this book, we have sought to look through the lens of multiple perspectives. We have asked ourselves, What responsibilities do district administrators have as they write policy and set the direction of the school district? How does the school leader promote the infusion of these characteristics within the individual school community? What role do parents have and how do schools ensure their voices are heard? What do individual teachers need to do as they work on the front lines juggling stan-

PREFACE

dards, evaluation processes, and systems, and managing the other myriad responsibilities they face? And lastly, where do our students fit, what parts do they play in learning, applying, and integrating these characteristics into their daily lives, both now and in the future?

The work is critical. We have taken to heart the charge to go out and make a difference. It is our belief that we must make an attempt to provide all who would work in our schools the tools required to help them get started. Not only can we impact our children's achievement of the standards that we as a nation so highly value, but we can make a lasting impact on the dispositional development of our children. We can equip them with those deeply meaningful attributes that are seemingly lacking in our society. We can help them become kinder, gentler, more civil, compassionate, and courageous beings. And, after all, isn't that what it is really all about?

1

CREATING A CLIMATE

MAKING THE CASE

In recent years, our nation has witnessed an alarming upswing in the number of incidents reflecting a lack of civility, compassion, and even courageous behaviors and actions. In the workplace, in politics, and even in our classrooms, there are glaring examples of people who fail to demonstrate acts of kindness and care for others—people who have forgotten how to or fail to share kind words with others. There are examples of individuals who fear doing what is necessary even when it frightens them. There are those who are discourteous and fail to demonstrate politeness in seemingly uncomplicated situations. However, the picture is not entirely bleak. In fact, there are also those who demonstrate extraordinary acts of compassion and courage and those who are great examples of civility, even in the face of adversity or intensely difficult circumstances.

Our current political landscape might be one of the best and most extreme examples of incivility, hate mongering and uncompassionate behaviors. *Dirty politics*, *mudslinging*—describes the unethical practices politicians and their operators use to gain political advantages over their opponents. This has increasingly led to scandals and salacious front page news stories. Many of those stories have ended or at the very least, severely crippled campaigns and destroyed lives. In fact, there are reports that civility has sharply declined since President Barack Obama took office in 2009

(Levine, 2010). Political radio and television talk shows fuel incivility and use inciting language against the opposing parties. While many believe civility is important in politics, it is often missing from debates and political discourse in our country.

In the early 1980s, "going postal" in the workplace quickly became the phrase of choice to describe when one's emotionality was high and fueled by a dearth of compassion, civility, and courage. While the phrase is now often used in jest, it speaks to a serious issue in our workplace environments—an issue that yearns for individuals to demonstrate the courage to walk away from a situation or even approach a situation with kindness and consideration for others. While going postal is an extreme example, there are other less obvious examples of individuals lacking courage, demonstrating incivility, and failing to show compassion for other people. For example, we see television shows and movies depicting in-office antics and sabotage—individuals who will engage in unethical, illegal, and unconscionable behavior to gain advancement. One might ask, "Is this life imitating art or vice versa?"

Our classrooms have also unfortunately become a place where students are failing to demonstrate these attributes. Attention to bullying, for example, has grown exponentially over the past several years. Traditional or cyberbullying has become so prevalent, it has forced families to move, students to transfer to different schools, and in some extreme cases, students have committed suicide or other acts of violence. We see increasing numbers of students engaging in deplorable behaviors and actions against one another. Schools across the country, in an effort to stem the tide of bullying, have poured funds and resources into anti-bullying campaigns. Celebrities and athletes participate in public service announcements. Schools are forced to limit technology in schools for fear of improper usage by students. Yet, the problems persist.

These problems, issues, and concerns are troublesome, but there are tremendous examples of individuals who have demonstrated heroics in the face of danger. There are schools that have taken a proactive approach to disengage students from behaving badly. For instance, Nebraska Law 79-725 mandates that the Commissioner of Education provide suggestions for character education for all schools in the state. This state instituted civility and responsibility training programs for elementary and middle school children. Other states such as Florida and Virginia are training teachers and paraprofessionals to work with students in response to a perceived demoralization among fellow students. A summary of all states' efforts can be found at http://www.character.org/wp-content/uploads/What-States-Are-Doing

.pdf. In the workplace, many businesses are instituting civility training for employees in an effort to create a more harmonious work environment. All these programs and efforts are designed to train and teach children and adults to behave in a more appropriate manner—to not only be civil, but to also be compassionate and kind.

In the news, there are stories of courage and compassion peppered among the numerous other scandalous stories. We often hear of courage in the face of danger when our country suffers the horrors of school shootings, as was the case in Sandy Hook where 20 students and 6 teachers died at the hands of a troubled young man. However, from that tragedy came many instances of teachers who sacrificed their lives to save their students. These teachers and administrators valiantly demonstrated what it means to be courageous and compassionate. This was also the case in the story of a secretary who talked a gunman down and potentially saved hundreds of students' lives in a school just outside of Atlanta, Georgia. Her demonstration of courage, compassion, and composure was awe inspiring. These are just a few examples of such tragic events we see in our national news far too frequently.

Obviously, we are not suggesting that these are the only ways to show such values. We are, however, suggesting that these are some extreme examples that have been captured in the media. While these stories will be an unfortunate part of our nation's history, there are other ways in which we can demonstrate everyday civility, care, and compassion toward and for others. In an effort to cultivate these values and positive behaviors in our children, we may need to begin with this question: where did these extraordinary people learn to be compassionate, courageous and civil?

Certainly, it is easy to immediately suggest that parents are responsible for teaching children how to demonstrate care for others, face fears, and be courteous. While we agree, we also pose these questions: What happens when parents don't teach those skills, attributes, and behaviors? What happens when students in our K–12 classroom exhibit behaviors, actions, and, in many instances, values that compromise citizenry and responsibility? Who is responsible for teaching civility, compassion, and courage in our K–12 classrooms? We suggest these responsibilities lie at all of our feet.

In the classroom, it is the teacher who is responsible for engaging students in lessons, discussions, reflections, and experiences to foster a valuing of these characteristics. It is the teacher who facilitates learning to internalize how these attributes will add to the quality to their learning and their lives. In a broader context it is also the administrators, school leaders, counselors and others who have the premium responsibility of instructional leadership and facilitator of learning in his or her school. These leaders, teachers, administrators, policy makers, and others are accountable for the learning that happens in the classroom and the school. We suggest that all responsible persons should take a proactive approach to teaching and facilitating social and emotional learning which includes the development of such skills as civility, compassion, and courage.

Over the past two decades we have seen educational policies gradually shift and change in order to reflect more on acquisition of traditional content areas and to assess the degree to which all students have mastered that content. High stakes testing is used to make budgetary, personnel, and resources decisions in schools across the nation. During this time, and perhaps even before the *No Child Left Behind Act*, policy makers and others have managed to drain civility, compassion, and courage from everyday classroom instruction. We have grown to become an educational system that is almost solely focused on academics at the expense of teaching to the whole child. We submit that civility, compassion, and courage are absolutely essential to foster good citizenship—to encourage and motivate students to action—to take on the perspectives of others, and to see how they can become productive members in an ever changing global community. We also recognize and acknowledge that there are many others that may be promoted as well.

To be fair, teachers are struggling to meet new standards, policies, and practices. Often times, teachers will complain they have little to no time to fully implement changes before the next big thing comes along. As these changes occur, the tendency is to go with the flow, which often leads us away from those perspectives and ideals that will promote good citizenship. Many schools over the past several years have adopted character education programs. A school's approach may include identifying the word of the day and defining it during the morning announcements. One might see the word posted in hallways and classrooms. Yet, students have most likely *not* been authentically engaging in experiences, opportunities, or exercises to begin valuing and internalizing the character word of the day or month. These students are basically at what Krathwohl, Bloom, and Masia (1964), in their Affective Hierarchy, called the *attending level*. At this level one is simply made aware or becomes aware of something. Students do not have an authentic and lived understanding, nor do they truly value its worth in their lives.

In our theory, the Model of Influence (MOI), we suggest that students are at a level of developing a consciousness about the concept, subject, or topic. The basic idea of the MOI is to move from consciousness to action and embracing influence. The Model of Influence will be discussed in greater detail later in this chapter, as it provides a framework for teaching and promoting civility, compassion, and courage in the classroom.

DEFINING THE ATTRIBUTES

First, civility is defined as politeness, courteous behavior, or speech. Certainly, there are times in the classroom where students could behave or speak in a more polite, courteous manner. But consistent implementation of civil behavior goes much deeper than that. In a time where much of our interactions happen via the computer—through social media sites and such, we ask: could it be that our children and adults are losing our ability to communicate in a polite manner? Are we becoming civilly illiterate? An internet search will reveal that there are thousands of entries online related to civility. Recovery of our lost abilities to become civil and reestablishment of civility as a priority has become a challenge from the K–12 classroom to the workplace. Clearly, there is trouble in the land.

Second, compassion is defined as having a concern for others. Too often we are bombarded with images, stories, and news through the media and other similar outlets that highlight how insensitive people are to one another. Reality TV shows often depict and glorify the worse human behavior imaginable. Occasionally, the nightly news or other programs will highlight interest stories of individuals engaging and demonstrating great compassion. Studies for the past two decades or more have revealed a correlation between the images and stories we view through media and the effects those stories have on children and young adults. This book is not as much about how those negative images filtrate into the outward behavior of the children in our classroom. It is more about what types of messages and what kinds of teaching we can bring into our classrooms to demonstrate the value of caring for and about other people.

Third, courage is the strength to do something which frightens you. This can sometimes be misconstrued as simply an act of self-service. In this context, we see courage as something deeper and greater; we see a boldness that takes the sometimes tentative step forward even in the face of great adversity. Courage in our K–12 classrooms is multi-faceted and can manifest in many ways. It might be simply demonstrating courage to ask questions about the content, the processes used in the classroom, or even about school policies. It could mean showing the courage to seek a greater understanding of material presented. It might also mean calling upon one's inner courage to advocate for oneself or someone else in need.

We do not suggest that these are the only three attributes missing from our K–12 curriculum. Certainly there are others that can be promoted, encouraged, and integrated into every day lessons. What we are suggesting is that these attributes hold a great significance to how we build relationships with others, see ourselves as greater than ourselves, and care about other people and the greater society. These attributes can also serve as a foundation for other attributes to be integrated later.

Finally, we suggest that we, as educators, move beyond a point where we are obsessed with covering all the content at the expense of our students engaging in real and relevant educational experiences. We should maximize students' purpose and potential to be difference makers—to take action and embrace the influence and the impact they can make in the lives of others, for themselves, and for the good of the greater community. In many ways it is using these, and perhaps other social-emotional competencies, to do as suggested by Marian Wright Edelman when she urged us to leave the community and world a better place than we found it (Wright, 1992). But, the question that might remain is this: how do we, as educators, promote and implement social-emotional learning and leave the world better for others? The next chapter is the beginning of organizing a process—a theoretical framework to address that question posed above.

REFERENCES

Character education—What states are doing. (2006). Retrieved August 4, 2014, from http://www.character.org/wp-content/uploads/What-States-Are-Doing.pdf

Edelman, Marian Wright (1992). *The measure of our success: A letter to my children and yours.* New York: Beacon Press.

Krathwohl, D., Bloom, B., & Masia, B. (1964). *Taxonomy of educational objectives, Book 2: Affective domain.* New York: Longman.

Levine, P. (2010). Teaching and learning civility. *New Directions for Higher Education*, 152. pp. 11–17. DOI:10.1002/he.407.

2

A THEORETICAL FRAMEWORK: THE MODEL OF INFLUENCE

In 1964 Krathwohl, Bloom, and Masia developed a theory of affective development that characterizes how one moves along a continuum of internalizing various schemes, constructs, ideas, and experiences (Krathwohl et al., 1964). It is often represented in hierarchical stages that include attending, responding, valuing, organizing, and characterizing or internalizing. At each stage the learner, in this instance, becomes more invested in the concept and grows a much deeper desire to maximize their understanding. Krathwohl is right to suggest that a student's learning is compromised when he or she fails to receive or attend to the teaching. In order for a student to maximize the learning, he or she must go much deeper in his or her understanding. Consequently, the teacher must ensure that this understanding takes place. The Affective Hierarchy served as a foundation for the Model of Influence (MOI) that we developed. Our model is a framework to guide how to move from developing a consciousness to taking action and embracing your influence to affect change.

As we delve into promoting civility, compassion, and courage in the classroom, we integrate the teaching and learning and show how one might use this model as a framework to move students from simple awareness of an attribute or value, to an internalization of how these attributes affect one's life and one's learning. In the context of promoting and teaching civility, compassion, and courage, at each stage, the student becomes increasingly invested in the learning—ultimately leading to action and embracing influence to impact the lives of others in a positive way.

THE MODEL OF INFLUENCE

Our Model of Influence (figure 2.1), shown below, is a theoretical framework that defines four levels to facilitate when developing and teaching value-oriented concepts leading to one taking action and embracing the influence they have to make a difference in the lives, hearts, and humanity of others. It is important to note that the MOI is not an add-on to the instruction or school's curriculum. The model is a framework that should be integrated into to the curriculum and across content areas. While we present civility, compassion, and courage—the 3C's, as the focal point for this book, the MOI framework can be used as a model, a framework to teach and promote other attributes such as gratitude, taking initiative, honesty, and many others.

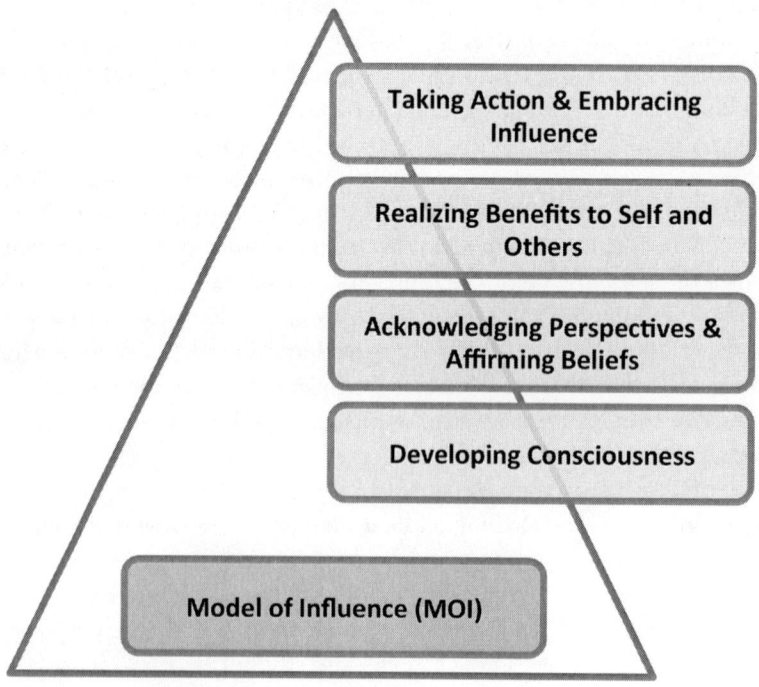

Figure 2.1.

A THEORETICAL FRAMEWORK

We propose that the first level to consider in our Model of Influence is to *develop consciousness* for a concept in order to promote learning of the attribute or value. This requires one to move beyond the act of passive learning to active learning. It also means that both the student and teacher must embrace their roles as learning-follower and learning-leader in the classroom. It is at this level that the concept becomes real and meaningful for all learners. This is the level that builds upon an individual's curiosity and interest to learn more. It might also be the level at which one begins to grapple with his or her own cognitive dissonance about certain topics, ideas, or perspectives. In a K–12 setting, both the teacher and the student need to experience this level so that both find meaning and relevance in the topic.

The second level is to foster acceptance of the new idea and awareness that various perspectives exist—*acknowledging perspectives and affirming beliefs*. When building upon the challenges which compromise one's current thinking, one begins to acknowledge other perspectives have relevancy and meaning. This might occur even if those ideals, principles, or beliefs are in opposition to one's own value system. Accepting that differences exist to be further examined can often affirm, extend, challenge, or even change one's thinking. It is important to note that we are not proposing that the purpose is to change how another person thinks. We are, however, proposing to offer them other ideas to consider or engage in perspective taking to deepen their knowledge of how others may interpret, analyze, and reflect on various concepts, thoughts, statements, and ideas.

The third level is *realizing the benefit to oneself and to others*. As with the last level, the idea is to build upon the knowledge gained and insight discovered and shared. It is often times far easier for humans to identify how something will benefit self. What has sometimes become difficult is for us to recognize the relevance of our lives to others. In other words, how are each of our lives connected to others' lives, and how can we use our lives to be productive, compassionate, caring members of mankind? How can we use our talents, knowledge, skills, and lives to support and serve others? When we take the time to examine the perspectives of others, witness their struggles and successes, it can empower one to see beyond self and find ways to advocate and help others. It also affords opportunities to enter the last level—*taking action and embracing influence* we have to make a difference. The idea of this third level is to engage in discourse, discussion, reflection, and yes, explicitly, authentically teach each attribute.

Taking action and embracing influence represents the highest level of the framework because it requires one to take some courageous steps to initiate necessary change—steps that might seem daunting, challenging, foolish, or daring. Each previous level requires one to "do something"—that doing something might be study more, ask more questions, engage in more discussion, do more research. This level of *action and embracing influence* encourages one to develop and seek a sustainable response to an issue, problem, or concern. It might also be difficult because many individuals may not necessarily see themselves as difference makers, nor might they recognize the gifts and talents they have to offer.

This level requires one to retreat from the fear that stifles creativity, flexibility, organization, and productivity, and move toward embracing those attributes to galvanize movements, initiatives, service-mindedness, and action. It is at this level of influence and action that the value system is manifested into behaviors that exemplify civility, courage, and compassion. Throughout the remainder of this book, elements of this model will be evident. As we contemplate the state of emergency in our educational system, it is vital that we seek every opportunity to support our students and help them develop the skills, dispositions, and social-emotional competencies with vigor and determination.

PURPOSE AND IMPORTANCE

We purport that while we spend copious amounts of instructional time on teaching math, science, reading, and such, we should also spend some time on promoting and teaching children to care for and about each other, to act and speak in a courteous manner, and to do what is right and good even in the face of fear. We further assert that our futures depend on this reframing of our classroom priorities. We believe that our mission as human beings is to leave the world a bit better as a result of our having been a part of humanity. What better way to increase one's circle of influence than by seeking to promote civility, compassion, and courage in our children and our future?

In subsequent chapters, we will consider various aspects of civility, compassion, and courage in the K–12 setting. In the next chapter, the literature on the three concepts of civility, compassion, and courage will be explored. This chapter will address current research and classroom applications. Considerations for teachers will also be discussed.

Chapter 3 provides the current research and some classroom applications for consideration. Chapters 4, 5, and 6, provide what we call "stories." These stories provide context for reflection and further discourse. Chapters 7, 8, and 9 offer example lesson plans for grades ranges: K–2, 3–5, 6–8, and 9–12 as it relates to each attribute. Each chapter will end with discussion questions and reflections to consider. Finally, chapter 10 will address the role of school administrators, leaders, counselors, and other support personnel in the effort to promote civility, compassion, and courage. We hope the reader will reflect on the suggested strategies presented to begin program implementation.

REFERENCE

Krathwohl, D., Bloom, B., & Masia, B. (1964). *Taxonomy of educational objectives, Book 2: Affective domain*. New York: Longman.

③

CURRENT RESEARCH AND CLASSROOM APPLICATIONS

WHAT DOES THE LITERATURE SAY?

In chapter 1 we cited numerous examples of incidents reflecting a lack of civility, compassion, and courageous behaviors. We alluded to our political landscape, our workplace environments and our classrooms as arenas in which uncivil, uncompassionate, and uncourageous behaviors abound. In short, we attempted to build a case for the need for critical attention to the teaching of these skills within the K–12 classroom. We assert that our nation's health is dependent on the degree to which we are successful.

As we continue to explore these behaviors, our attention now turns to the literature and existing resources for each attribute. We will explore the promotion of these behaviors in our current educational system. In addition, we will attempt to strengthen our case for infusing our instructional time with lessons on civility, compassion and courage. Finally, we will more deeply discuss the role of teachers as well as the role of parents.

A Brief Review: Civility

Civility, defined as politeness, courteous behavior, or speech, can also be viewed as maintaining social harmony or demonstrating respect for the humanity of an individual (Wilkins, Caldarella, Crook-Lyon, and Young,

2010). From its Latin roots, *civis* (citizen) and *civitas* (city), the connection between civility and the maintenance of a functioning society is made clear.

Other words that might be used to define civility include the characteristics of consideration, gentility, respect, caring, and looking beyond selfishness (Hinckley, 2000). In his recent book, *The Civility Solution*, Forni suggests that the opposite of civility is rudeness (2008); he further asserts that the damage caused by another's rudeness can result in stress, the erosion of self-esteem, problems in relationship, and escalation into violence. The questions begs, how have our schools attempted to address this critical skill, and what have been the results of such attempts?

Public education has long been associated with the charge to nurture a civil society. Serving to improve society is a pivotal hoped-for outcome of our educational system. The recently published National Council for the Social Studies *National Curriculum Standards for Social Studies: A Framework for Teaching, Learning, and Assessment* (Herczog, 2010), includes civic competence as a central goal. Further, The *Ten Themes of the National Curriculum Standards for Social Studies: A Framework for Teaching, Learning, and Assessment* identifies civic ideals and practices as one of the major themes. According to the stated themes, social studies programs should "include experiences that provide for the study of the ideals, principles, and practices of citizenship in a democratic republic" (Ten Themes of the National Curriculum Standards for Social Studies: A Framework for Teaching, Learning, and Assessment [Herczog, 2010]). One can conclude that the language is included in the standards; however, how are the intentions of the standards reflected in schools? And more importantly, how are the standards reflected in our students?

Most would suggest that incivility has not only increased in society as a whole, but also in the schools. Little empirical evidence exists that actually examines the actual levels or changes in civil behaviors over time (Wilkins et al., 2010). Walker, Ramsey, and Gresham define antisocial behavior as hostility and aggression toward others and society (as cited in Wilkins et al., 2010). They suggest that these misbehaviors can lead to more serious behaviors and that, if not treated, an antisocial pattern identified in the school years can lead to an antisocial personality disorder in adulthood.

Gargarino suggests that youth violence can, in many cases, be attributed to personal and familial dysfunction, but can also be perpetuated by negative school environments; unattended, the result is often violence and crime (as cited in Wilkins et al., 2010). According to the National Center for School Statistics, during the 2005–2006 school year, 86 percent of public schools reported at least one theft, violent crime, or other crime in a school setting (as cited in Wilkins et al., 2010). Where is the good news in this?

Finding successful programs with a focus on teaching civility is difficult. Perhaps one of the best go-to places for resources is *Teaching Tolerance* (www.teachingtolerance.org), a project of the Southern Poverty Law Center. This free resource provides a monthly magazine with lesson plan ideas on such topics as bullying, combating bias, abuse, addressing aggression, and other issues relating to civility. In addition, the subscriber has access to a variety of free film kits, and other classroom resources. Research on the effectiveness of these materials has not been noted, but anecdotally, in the authors' opinions, teachers have received and utilized the information positively.

Sociodrama has also been cited as a possible way to address uncivil behaviors, such as bullying. Cossa (2006) uses role play activities to generate discussions about bullying behaviors and appropriate responses. Parents are invited to witness the work, and students who participate are more likely to seek support when being bullied as a result of their participation. In addition to bullying behavior, Cossa also addresses problem solving and anger management using civil means.

The Safe & Civil Schools Series created by Randy Sprick, is a collection of practical materials designed to improve safety and civility across all school settings. Responsible and respectful behaviors are targeted through a variety of materials designed for school personnel. Effective use of Safe & Civil Schools programs reportedly results in reductions in suspensions and expulsions, increases in connectedness, and perceptions of increased safety and civility. The authors of this program offer a comprehensive professional development program with flexible training features.

Finally, a search for programs that address civility led the authors to several programs addressing civility on college campuses and/or the workplace. Moreno Valley College has developed a training manual titled *Civility in the Workplace* that addresses such topics as work ethic, conflict resolution, effective communication and negotiation, as well as several other related areas. The University of Missouri has developed a website that serves to promote civility; this site contains a "Civility Toolbox" that contains tips, articles, and other resources.

Clearly, it is evident that there exists a critical need for infusing instruction on civil behavior into the curriculum. Reaching from the standards to the lesson plan is challenging, yet the potential benefits are unrealized. In the next section, we will explore the literature on compassion, and the resulting need to teach this critical attribute in our schools.

A Brief Review: Compassion

Earlier, we defined compassion as having a concern for others. The word compassion originates from English, Anglo-French or Late Latin, from the word *compati* to sympathize. Compassion involves both a sympathetic consciousness of another's distress and a desire to alleviate that distress. According to Seppala (2013), compassion is different from empathy, although the two are often confused. Seppala suggests that empathy is the visceral or emotional experience of another's feelings.

Compassion begins with the emotional response but adds an authentic desire to help, making it much more powerful. Compassion actually combines empathy (emotional response) with altruism (action benefitting another). In a recent study conducted by researchers from the University of Wisconsin, taking a course in compassion can prompt higher levels of altruistic behavior (Weng et al., 2013). In other words, compassion can be cultivated. How is compassion manifested in the school environment?

The Compassionate Schools Initiative has identified ten principles of a compassionate school ("Compassionate schools"):

- Focus on culture and climate in the school and community.
- Train and support all staff regarding trauma and learning.
- Encourage and sustain open and regular communication for all.
- Develop a strengths based approach in working with students and peers.
- Ensure discipline policies are both compassionate and effective (Restorative Practices).
- Weave compassionate strategies into school improvement planning.
- Provide tiered support for all students based on what they need.
- Create flexible accommodations for diverse learners.
- Provide access, voice, and ownership for staff, students and community.
- Use data to
  - identify vulnerable students, and
  - determine outcomes and strategies for continuous quality improvement.

Although the list could easily be applied to areas other than compassion, such as diversity, culturally responsive teaching, and meeting the needs of students with disabilities, it provides a place from which to begin dialogue on teaching compassion in the schools. What other evidence exists to support teaching compassion?

The Washington State Office of Superintendent of Public Instruction (OSPI) has made available to the public a comprehensive resource for schools titled *The Heart of Learning and Teaching: Compassion, Resiliency, and Academic Success*. This 246 page handbook discusses such topics as trauma, resiliency, responsiveness, compassion fatigue, emotional and behavioral self-regulation, and competencies of personal agency, social, and academic skills. As part of the Compassionate Schools Initiative, training, guidance, referral, and technical assistance is available to schools wishing to develop a compassionate schools infrastructure. A primary goal is to keep students engaged and learning through a supported healthy climate and culture within the school.

The Compassionate Action Network International supports compassion initiatives on a global basis (http://compassionateaction.org). The organization partners with schools and universities by sharing case studies, curriculum, resources, and stories from institutions seeking to embed compassion into every aspect of the learning process. The Children's Charter for Compassion is an example of one such resource. The purpose of the charter is to provide a means for children and those around them to understand how to treat themselves and others with love, kindness, and compassion. Downloadable activity books are suggested that provide children with ideas for acting in a compassionate manner.

The Compassion Games (http://compassiongames.org) originated in Louisville, Kentucky, when the mayor asked citizens to perform acts of service in the community during a one-week period. During that week, more than 90,000 acts of service were recorded. The website provides opportunities to sign up for three different kinds of games: Secret Agents of Compassion, Random Acts of Kindness, and Service Projects. In order to "play" as a secret agent of compassion, young participants receive a daily e-mail during two weeks in September urging them to commit compassionate acts and "report" these. Acts are recorded for other participants to view. The website also provides shared stories of compassion from around the globe.

As with civility, the case for embedding compassion in the school curriculum is strong, especially in light of the research indicating that compassion can be cultivated. It stands to reason that our ever-growing population and the diverse nature of our schools demands that we seek to understand one another. Surely we can grow students who demonstrate both empathy (experiencing another's emotion) and altruism (acting upon that feeling in a beneficial way) to make this a more kind and gentle world. In the next section, we will dig more deeply into the attribute, courage, and how it is currently addressed through our schools.

A Brief Review: Courage

A discussion about the meaning of courage cannot take place without the image of the cowardly lion from the classic film *The Wizard of Oz*, whose sole pursuit was that of gaining courage. The lack of bravery was evident in a variety of scenes in which the lion shrank from any dangerous situations that presented themselves. From the movie, it may seem that courage is synonymous with bravery; we assert that courage is much more.

In chapter 1, we suggested that courage was deeper and greater, a boldness that takes the sometimes tentative step forward even in the face of great adversity. The Latin *cor* which means "heart," suggests that courage is a metaphor for inner strength. Certainly the cowardly lion was actually seeking that which would arise from within to help him champion and protect Dorothy and friends, even when facing such evil opponents as the flying monkeys and the wicked witch. Let's take a look at what this looks like in our schools.

In a recent study, Andrew Martin suggests that teaching students how to bring courage into their daily school lives, greatly improves their learning, performance, and level of engagement (2011). Martin examines several approaches to schoolwork, including courage; other approaches include confidence, avoidance, and helplessness. Courage is defined by Martin as "a perseverance through academic difficulty in the face of fear" (Martin, 2011, p. 146). Martin concludes that courage is as effective an approach as confidence in impacting achievement in literacy and numeracy, particularly in the face of fear and anxiety. By shifting students' focus to controllable elements such as effort and goal setting, students will develop an increased sense of empowerment.

Expeditionary Learning (EL) is a model serving over 150 public schools in 30 states by targeting primarily low income urban and rural communities. This model asserts that academic success positively correlates with well-developed, non-cognitive skills. Chief program academic officer of EL, Ron Berger, states that the character strength at the center of the model's success is courage (2013). According to Berger, "the culture and structures . . . are designed to encourage taking risks—risks with difficult texts or math problems, risks with questions, discussions, and presentations in class, risks with artistic and athletic challenges, and risks to cross boundaries and support others socially" (Berger, 2013, p. 15).

Berger cultivates academic as well as community courage. Lessons intentionally build academic courage through clear learning targets with public reflections, discussion protocols compelling taking risks and sharing ideas, and debriefs that include public affirmations of success and problems. Community courage is taught through working on a small advisory group that meets daily. The group members hold one another accountable, compliment and critique classmates, and work to speak up in their neighborhoods, showing kindness and vulnerability. Berger states that courage is foundational to building a more responsive culture.

Another source for the teaching of courage is the series entitled Good Character (www.goodcharacter.com). This website provides lessons for students in grades K–12 on a variety of topics in addition to courage. These include fairness/justice, diligence, integrity, responsibility, and other lesson topics. Although there is just one lesson on the topic of courage for middle school and one for high school, the site provides numerous other resources including articles, links to other organizations, and opportunities for community involvement.

The search for research and resources on teaching courage yielded fewer results than the other attributes addressed in this book. Perhaps a case for teaching courage might pose the strongest sense of obligation to our children. Certainly, we are in desperate need of having students stand up for themselves in the face of fear, anxiety, and other adversity. Our schools cry out for those who will face down the bullies, for those who take the tougher yet more rewarding and productive route, for those who will find it within themselves to look inwardly for heart and inner strength despite the odds. Could it be that finding meaningful ways to instill courage might be the most significant work of all?

ADVICE TO TEACHERS

In chapter 1 we acknowledged that teachers are often bombarded with new ideas, curricula, programs, and the latest trending concept with claims of magically changing the way in which students learn and teachers teach. We offer no fairy dust to sprinkle and do not suggest there is a magical solution. What we suggest, however, is a common sense approach to educating children—an approach that is evidenced by the link between academic performance and social and emotional learning. It was John Dewey who suggested that our schools are a reflection of our societies and should work in ensure children are prepared for a future of learning and living.

Dewey stated:

> The common needs and aims demand a growing interchange of thought and grounding unity of sympathetic feeling. Upon the playground, in game and sport, social organization takes place spontaneously and inevitably. There is

something to do, some activity to be carried on, requiring natural divisions of labor, selection of leaders and followers, mutual cooperation and emulation. Upon the ethical side, the tragic weakness of the present school is that it endeavors to prepare future members of the social order in a medium in which the conditions of the social spirit eminently wanting. (Dewey, 1956, p. 25–26)

Therefore, it is the job of school to attend to the full growth and development of each child—to ensure that every child has an opportunity to become a learner who thinks, feels, and acts in a way that represents the better of society. Likewise in our classrooms, these small societies and communities are often the richest soil that will fertilize the seedlings into blossoming flowers with strong roots in values, behaviors and actions— characteristics that should be as celebrated as reading, writing, and math.

A student who is compassionate, who cares about himself and others, and who understands how to speak and engage in polite discourse will gain skills that reach far and beyond the classroom walls. Do we as K–12 teachers not want our students to be full engaging members of society, or are we so concerned about their reading achievement that we negate their humanity?

Certainly, we do not purport that it is solely the responsibility of teachers to deliver instruction on these concepts, nor are we advocating that there should be a dogmatic emphasis on academic achievement. What we are suggesting is in our K–12 classrooms, teachers must move away from blaming parents for students misbehaving in the classrooms, to taking some responsibility for teaching and integrating character-building experiences, content, and activities into their daily instructional plans.

Researchers from California State University-Fresno conducted a study to examine the link between high achieving schools and character education programs. What they found supports the idea that teachers can be instrumental in supporting students' acknowledgement and later valuing of character-building traits that then lead to those students exemplifying those attributes throughout their lives. Their research found several indicators of schools with both solid character education programs and high levels of student achievement (Benninga, Berkowitz, Kuehn, and Smith, 2006). Those indicators include the following:

- *Clean and secure environment.* Taking pride in ensuring that the school grounds and the physical appearance portray a sense of safety, care for others and your surroundings.
- *Adults act as models of values and virtues.* Students need to see adults modeling compassion, civility, care, respect, compassion, perspective taking, and other such traits and attributes.

- *High student engagement in school–community projects.* Students need to have varied and meaningful ways to engage in their communities through volunteerism, service-learning, and other such coordinated events.
- *Promoting positive relationships.* This indicator speaks not only to the relationships that teachers have with students, but also the relationships that teachers, parents, administrators, and community representatives and partners have with each other and the school to create rich learning and social-emotional opportunities for students. For example, schools across the country engage in Family Literacy night or other special events to foster the sense of a caring community.

These types of events and programming allow teachers, in particular, the opportunity to learn more about who their students are and what their family dynamics consist of. Further, teachers can learn how they might approach individualized learning, and how they might create a space to have discourse with parents about building character through school-home connections.

There is a ponderous amount of research which supports the claims that there is a link between high achieving schools and the integration of character building curriculum into a rich learning environment for students. To ensure the whole student is supported, it is important for teachers to widen their view about their role as instructional leaders in the classroom and find ways to support and develop students' character and social and emotional competencies while also focusing on their academic achievement. In doing so, teachers will support the development of the whole child.

In our Model of Influence, presented in chapter 2, we assert that there is a hierarchy—a framework to help move from awareness to action. While we agree with the research claims discussed previously, we suggest additional indicators for teachers to consider as they struggle with how to incorporate or find the time to focus on such skills. Clearly, there are many schools across the country that are doing this kind of work while experiencing great success.

We add three additional considerations for teachers:

- *Develop integrated instruction.* This allows teachers to bring the standards and the character trait into focus. In later chapters we provide some sample or example lessons for K–12 classrooms. However, the research indicates that when teachers teach character traits through content standards, the overall school environment improves, there is increased academic achievement and there is an increase in the social relationships and emotional prowess of students. The instruction might begin with simply defining, identifying, or discussing a particular trait, but it should not end there. Teachers must find ways for students to demonstrate their understanding, self-identify when they are demonstrating that trait, recognize the trait in others, and help them make greater meaning of how that trait is connected to a real-world situation.

- *Accept the role of influencer.* Like it or not, teachers are the great influencers. There is great power that comes with the role. For most adults, they may not remember how to solve an equation with a distributive property, but they do remember the math teacher who never gave up on them and worked with them until they understood how to solve that difficult problem. They remember the compassion and care that teacher modeled and as a result, have good memories about their school experiences. Likewise, some adults remember the frustrated, seemingly impatient, and uncivil teachers they encountered throughout their schooling. Unfortunately, those teachers were as influential as the great teachers.
- *Remember the whole child.* Over the past three decades our nation's educational-political system has focused much attention on standards, achievement, standardized tests, and competiveness among other industrialized countries. We must remember the mission of education and teaching is to promote more than global competiveness; it is also to teach students how to be global citizens who demonstrate care and compassion, respect and civility, and perseverance and courage. It is our responsibility as teachers to remember that our students are complex, unique, and have interesting perspectives, values and life experiences—all of which guide how they operate in the world and with others. In remembering the whole child, we must respond to their emotional and social needs as much as we focus on their academic achievement. Arguably, it is often times those skills that will be as, or more beneficial, as they grow and develop throughout their lifespan.

In the next three chapters, the reader will be asked to read and reflect on stories that represent classroom dynamics across grade spans. Each story will suggest how a teacher seeks to weave civility, compassion, and courage into the framework of her academic instruction. The reader is encouraged to *deepen his/her awareness by developing consciousness*, the first level in the Model of Influence. In addition, we invite the reader to examine and *acknowledge his/her own perspectives and beliefs* (level two) concerning the characteristic, civility, compassion, or courage, and to begin to contemplate how instruction might encompass these critical attributes

RESOURCES

Teaching Tolerance (www.teachingtolerance.org)
Safe and Civil Schools (http://www.safeandcivilschools.com/)
Compassionate Action Network (http://compassionateaction.org/)
Compassion Games (http://compassiongames.org/)
Good Character (http://www.goodcharacter.com/)
University of Missouri Toolbox (http://civility.missouri.edu/toolbox.php)
Moreno Valley College—*Civility in the Workplace* (http://www.mvc.edu/files/ep-civility-workplace.pdf)
Washington State Office of Superintendent of Public Instruction (OSPI) Compassionate Schools—*The Heart of Learning and Teaching: Compassion, Resiliency, and Academic Success* (http://www.k12.wa.us/compassionateschools/)

REFERENCES

Benninga, J., Berkowitz, M. W., Kuehn, P., & Smith, K. (2006). Character and academics: What good schools do. *Phi Delta Kappan*, 87(6), 448.

Berger, R. (2013, October). Classes in courage. *Phi Delta Kappa*, 95(2).

Compassionate schools: The heart of learning and teaching. (n.d.). Retrieved from http://www.k12.wa.us/compassionateschools/

Cossa, M. (2006). How rude!: Using sociodrama in the investigation of bullying and harassing behavior and in teaching civility in educational communities. *Journal of Group Psychotherapy, Psychodrama & Sociometry*, 58(4), 182–194.

Dewey, J. (1956). *The school and society and the child and curriculum*. Chicago, IL: University of Chicago Press.

Forni, P. M. (2008). *The civility solution: What to do when people are rude*. New York: St. Martin's Griffin.

Herczog, M. M. (2010). Using the NCSS "National Curriculum Standards for Social Studies: A framework for teaching, learning, and assessment" to meet state social studies standards. *Social Education*, 74(4), 217–20.

Hinckley, G. B. (2000). *Standing for something: 10 neglected virtues that will heal our hearts and homes*. New York: Random House.

Martin, A. J. (2011). Courage in the classroom: Exploring a new framework predicting academic performance and engagement. *School Psychology Quarterly*, 26(2), 145–60.

Seppala, E. (2013). Science: The compassionate mind. *Compassion Journal*, Retrieved from http://compassionjournal.blogspot.com/

Weng, H. Y., Fox, A. S., Shackman, A. J., Stodola, D. E., Caldwell, J. K., Olson, M. C., & Davidson, R. J. (2013). Compassion training alters altruism and neural responses to suffering. *Psychological Science*, 24(7), 1171–180.

Wilkins, K., Caldarella, P., Crook-Lyon, R., & Young, K. (2010). Implications of civility for children and adolescents: A review of the literature. *Issues in Religion and Psychotherapy*, 33, 37–45.

4

BRINGING CIVILITY TO LIFE

In chapter 1, we posed these questions: Are we becoming civilly illiterate? Are we so endeared to our technology that we are losing our ability to communicate in a respectful and polite way? Can we recover, or perhaps, reclaim how we interact with one another in a positive way? Arguably, we are living in a time where our world is becoming increasingly more connected in some respects.

On the flip side, technology which connects us also seems to keep us disconnected and sometimes even terse with one another. It is imperative that in our K–12 classroom we use every available opportunity to teach students to be courteous, polite, and respectful of themselves and others, as well as appreciative of the contributions and significance we have in each other's lives. In our global connectedness, these skills will become more and more relevant and necessary. It will be essential that we are civilly literate and can express that in ways that demonstrate courteousness and politeness to one another.

In preparation for this chapter, we invite the reader to immerse himself/herself in one or more of the following scenarios. We have compiled what we call "stories" that are designed to be thought provoking in several ways by *developing consciousness*, our first level in the Model of Influence. In some stories, *acknowledging perspectives and affirming beliefs*, level two of the model, will be evident.

In some, you can see that students and teachers are realizing benefit to self and others, level three, and for others, students are beginning to *take action and embrace influence*, level four in the Model of Influence. As mentioned in chapter 2, however, *taking action and embracing influence* is a much more consistently demonstrated level than what is reflected in the stories we have written. For long term sustainability, intentional teaching must be carefully and purposefully embedded in daily delivery of our instruction.

As a reminder, these stories capitalize on incidental occurrences that result in purposeful actions on the part of the teacher. It is imperative that we remember to create space in our instruction for cultivating the attributes of civility, compassion, and courage, with the Model of Influence framework, regardless of the surrounding circumstances that may or may not occur.

These stories are written to be reflective of current classroom conditions in the designated grade level(s). They also suggest the complex situations and issues that affect teachers, auxiliary staff, and students. Finally, they are designed to serve as a tool for the reader as he/she contemplates the scenario and compares/contrasts it to his/her own classroom environment.

In keeping with our model, each story is designed to create awareness, and will be followed by an invitation to the reader to acknowledge perspectives and affirm beliefs, our second level in the Model of Influence. As mentioned earlier, hints of levels three and four will be noticed, but the foci for these chapters is levels one and two.

We ask the reader to think about aspects of each story, and we follow this with questions for reflection. Space is provided for the reader to record his/her thoughts, comments, and other responses. It is our belief that in order to move on to level three, *realizing benefit to self and others*, and to level four, *taking action and embracing influence*, we must first examine our own beliefs and responses to the characteristic being examined.

We start with Ms. Younger's kindergarten classroom, by describing what is occurring and Ms. Younger's response to her current circumstances. We will next pose questions for reflection, and ask the reader to briefly record his/her thoughts. After Ms. Younger, you will meet Mr. Lopez, a fifth grade teacher, then Mr. Smithers, an eighth grade teacher. Last, you will meet Mrs. Mathers, an eleventh grade science teacher. Each one faces different challenges, and each one responds to those challenges with the intention of embedding civility, compassion, and courage into his/her instruction.

MS. YOUNGER'S KINDERGARTEN CLASSROOM

In a kindergarten classroom of five- and six-year-old children, Ms. Younger is modeling and demonstrating to her students how to communicate and behave civilly. On this particular morning, the classroom feels hurried, excited, and overly stimulating. Parents are hustling children through the door with little time to say goodbye. Several children are crying and having great difficulty transitioning from their families to the classroom.

The school is also anticipating the arrival of an accrediting agent to visit and observe the kindergarten classroom at any time. Ms. Younger and the assistant teacher, Ms. Peterson, are themselves becoming a bit frazzled in all the chaos.

As the morning rush begins to slow down, Ms. Younger pounces on the opportunity to bring about some order to the chaotic morning. She takes a deep breath and begins to speak calmly to the children in a clear voice over the fray. She says, "Okay boys and girls! Let's put the toys away, please. Breakfast will be here soon." She quietly starts singing the "clean up song" and the children join in. She works with small groups of children putting toys away and organizing the room to prepare for breakfast, using "please" and "thank you" often, and the children sort toys into bins and place items on shelves.

As the children are cleaning up, breakfast arrives. Ms. Peterson calls the breakfast helpers over to help her prepare tables, settings, and such for each child. During breakfast both teachers are using this as a teachable moment to promote using polite language such as "please" and "thank you."

Think About, Ask, and Reflect

Ms. Younger's morning was fraught with numerous challenges, such as crying children, the anticipation of an external visit from an accrediting agent, as well as a general climate of overstimulation. For many teachers in the early grades, this is how most days begin.

Ask yourself:

- How did Ms. Younger and Ms. Peterson, who were a bit frazzled themselves, model politeness and courteous civil behavior?
- What impact did their behavior have on their students?
- What do you, the reader, believe were the perspectives and beliefs held by Ms. Younger and Ms. Peterson?

- What are your beliefs concerning the modeling of similar behaviors?
- How do your behaviors compare to Ms. Younger's when the day seems chaotic?
- How do you promote civil behavior through your behaviors with young children?
- What other attributes or values besides civility are represented?

Write your thoughts here:

_____
_____
_____
_____
_____
_____
_____

Summing Up Ms. Younger's Class Experience

In this story, Ms. Younger and Ms. Peterson modeled politeness, respect for others' feelings, and using positive language in various social situations. The children, in turn, used that which was modeled for them to assist each other. Ms. Younger then integrated the children's experience into a lesson on civility and compassion. Certainly, one lesson is not enough.

Students will need several lessons to fully develop an awareness and consciousness of why these skills are so critical to their lives and to the lives of others. It is the first level of the Model of Influence—*awareness followed by consciousness*. In this scenario it is the awareness of your surroundings, yours and other's perceptions, an alertness to, or sensitivity of, a particular situation, issue, or event that is a critical first step. It is through this understanding of the concept that one begins to have a state of mind about the concept and the importance of civility in his/her own life.

MR. LOPEZ'S FIFTH GRADE CLASSROOM

Mr. Lopez teaches in a school that represents a racial, ethnic, economic, and culturally diverse community in a large urban school district. Mr. Lopez has taught fifth grade for the past six years. Over the past several years, he has seen how rapidly the school has changed from serving predominately Latino and Hispanic students to a population of students that represents more than twelve countries with many students who are multilingual. He has also seen the difficulty that many teachers and students have with understanding the various traditions and religious customs that students from such varied backgrounds can bring.

As Mr. Lopez contemplates how he might use diversity to engage students in a service-learning project to deepen their understanding of one another, a student representing a more traditional group interrupts his thinking with a question. "Mr. Lopez," Samuel, the group's spokesperson says, "We were wondering why Amira wears a scarf to cover her head. We don't get it," he says with a smirk. Samuel's friends can be heard snickering in the background.

Mr. Lopez is perplexed by the lack of sensitivity the students show toward another student in class. What is most uncomfortable is the mortified and demoralizing expression that washes across Amira's face. Mr. Lopez quickly sees this as an opportunity to teach his students about not only sensitivity, but also respect for others traditions, cultures, and backgrounds. He also sees this as a natural connection to several social studies themes. First, though, Mr. Lopez needs to address the manner in which Samuel asked the question.

After explaining that we all have meaningful traditions and customs others may not understand, he explains that questions are good, but suggests considering another's feelings and perspectives when asking a question. Mr. Lopez asks Amira if she will explain why she wears her hijab. Although Amira is tentative to respond, after some coaching she explains why she covers her hair. Mr. Lopez then asks Samuel to explain why he wears a yarmulke and why that is important to Jewish customs.

Think About, Ask, and Reflect

In Mr. Lopez's community, rapid change over the last few years resulted in a very diverse student population. Mr. Lopez was cognizant of these changes and was seeking ways to bring his students together as a respectful community of learners. Although he was planning to launch a service learning project, his students demonstrated a lack of understanding regarding those who were different. Diversity often leads to misunderstandings and sometimes uncivil behavior.

Ask yourself:

- How did Mr. Lopez work toward helping his students respond to one another with respect?
- How did he use differences to promote civility?
- What perspectives and beliefs did Mr. Lopez's seemingly have?
- What is the supporting evidence for the assumed perspectives and beliefs?
- How might you promote civility when your classroom is characterized by a rapidly changing population?

Write your thoughts here:

_____
_____
_____
_____
_____
_____

Summing Up Mr. Lopez's Class Experience

Mr. Lopez was working to create a level of *awareness*, the first level in the Model of Influence with his students. The following day, Mr. Lopez introduced his students to their next project on Cultures and Customs Around the World by first asking them to engage in a think-pair-share about a silly or fun tradition their family has around the holidays. Then he asked them to discuss with their partner a special or unique custom that is a part of their culture. This was the beginning of a knowledge base for the students to build upon as they became more engaged in their project. Later, Mr. Lopez would assign several small research projects to help students immerse themselves in learning about different cultures and customs represented by their school, community and peers.

MR. SMITHERS' EIGHTH GRADE CLASSROOM

In an eighth grade language arts and social studies classroom, Mr. Smithers finds many of his students struggling with their civility toward each other. He finds they chide and frequently engage in thoughtless, hurtful comments about each other. Sadly, it appears that some of his students are unaware of how their comments are hurtful.

What is more troubling are the growing incidences of cyberbullying among certain students with a few targeted students. Mr. Smithers is determined to find a way to help his students learn how and why it is important to be civil by using more polite language and changing the way they engage with one another.

"Class, let's come together," Mr. Smithers says. "How many of you know what a PSA is?" A student in the front row of the class raises her hand. "Yes, Sara," he acknowledges. "A PSA is a public service announcement," she says, putting her hand down. "That's right, and can someone else tell me what PSAs are used for?" he asks. Another student toward the back of the class answers by saying, "People make them to deliver a message about something important."

"Exactly. I am going to show you three PSAs about different subjects."

Mr. Smithers shows the students PSAs for brushing teeth, drug awareness, and bullying. His idea is to introduce the concept of a PSA as well as use the last PSA as a catalyst for discussion on speaking and behaving in a polite and courteous manner—civility.

Mr. Smithers talks with his students about polite behavior and asks them to describe some examples of incivility and civility in the classroom and with each other. He also shows them news reports of the most horrific events that have occurred as a result of bullying. Mr. Smithers makes a point of connecting these incidents to individuals engaging in what they believed were perhaps harmless comments, pranks, and behavior that escalated into terrible events.

At first, the students are somewhat uncomfortable with offering examples and describing incidences when they had engaged in impolite behavior and actions. Many of them cite movies and TV shows that depict mean and intentionally hurtful behavior. This is a part of Mr. Smithers' goal. He wants students to have a certain level of discomfort in discussing how their own actions and behaviors might have affected someone else.

Think About, Ask, and Reflect

Mr. Smithers struggled with the lack of courteous behaviors exhibited by his eighth grade students. Although his instructional focus was meeting the course standards, he realized the importance of infusing his instruction with content related to the lack of civility.

Ask yourself:

- How did Mr. Smithers address his students' uncivil behaviors?
- In what ways did he link language arts content to teaching students the impact of their behaviors on others?
- What do you, the reader, believe were the perspectives and beliefs held by Mr. Smithers?
- How do your behaviors compare to Mr. Smithers' actions when students exhibit a lack of civil behavior?
- What are your beliefs concerning the modeling of similar behaviors?
- How do you promote civil behavior through your behaviors with young adolescents?

Write your thoughts here:

_____
_____
_____
_____
_____
_____
_____

Summing Up Mr. Smithers' Class Experience

After his discussion with his eighth grade language arts class, Mr. Smithers asked his students to create a PSA about the harmful effects of bullying and how to not be a bystander when someone is being bullied. The objective of this assignment was not only to engage students in learning to use technology to create a PSA, but also engage in group work and higher order thinking skills. He informed his students that they would plan, create, and present their PSA to the school during the next assembly.

Certainly, this one project is not the magic solution needed to resolve the issues Mr. Smithers observed among his students, but it allows students to deepen their understanding of how their actions and words can negatively impact others. It also allows the students to engage in an authentic learning experience to be used for greater purposes within the school and perhaps beyond.

In this scenario Mr. Smithers was planting the seeds of civility in his students. While researching and working together, Mr. Smithers modeled politeness for students as he deepened their learning about civility and assessed how students engaged with each other effectively. As students gain a certain *level of awareness*, they are engaging in the basic level of the Model of Influence. It is at this level that teachers can stir students' thinking about a concept, issue or event, or behavior.

MRS. MATHERS' ELEVENTH GRADE CLASSROOM

Jonah and Marcus are students in Mrs. Mathers' eleventh grade integrated science classroom. Over the first few weeks of school, they emerge as leaders among their peers. They smartly support struggling students when working in small groups by encouraging them and acting as role models for others.

Jonah and Marcus seem to truly value their roles in the classroom community. Mrs. Mathers is particularly pleased with their ability to see beyond themselves and redirect other students who sometimes say rude or unkind things to their peers. Mrs. Mathers wonders how she might encourage such social harmony and respect in all students and capitalize on the students who are already modeling civility.

Certainly, she does not want to lift up Jonah and Marcus as the sole representation of what it means to demonstrate civility. However, she knows from research that students who participate and engage in uncivil behavior can sometime escalate into more destructive patterns of behavior.

After much thought, Mrs. Mathers decides to involve Jonah and Marcus and get their input on her thinking. Asking them to stop by her class at lunch, they agree. After sharing her thoughts, the boys acknowledge their larger responsibility to their peers as perceived leaders in the school.

In conversation with Mrs. Mathers, they suggest that modeling good citizenship and promoting consciousness concerning the valuing of all students is part of their role as students and citizens. They suggest that Mrs. Mathers engage in daily dialog with all students about the meaning of applying the concepts of equity, equality, responsibility and justice they are learning in their government classes to the science classroom.

It is agreed that she will begin with a discussion about what citizenship actually means. Knowing that investing time in this discussion will greatly improve the climate of the classroom and possibly the school, Mrs. Mathers begins the class-wide conversation the next day.

Think About, Ask, and Reflect

Mrs. Mathers knew that applying the concept of citizenship to her integrated science class might be challenging for many students. Therefore, her first step was to set a foundation based on the many definitions and understandings of what citizenship means. Her goal was to help students build a classroom citizenry that translated into behaving and acting in a way that was highly productive and reflective of the greater society. Although Mrs. Mathers did not observe many uncivil behaviors, she decided to address citizenship.

Ask yourself:

- How did she apply the concept of citizenship to her integrated science class?
- What beliefs did Mrs. Mathers most likely hold?
- What was her approach to promoting civil behavior among her students?
- What do you see as your responsibility in the promotion of citizenship, even when the content may not traditionally lend itself to this?
- What might be your next steps?

Write your thoughts here:

_____
_____
_____
_____
_____
_____

Summing Up Mrs. Mathers' Class Experience

Helping her students develop a deep consciousness for the meaning of citizenship as it manifested itself in her classroom as well as the school, promoted internalization and the placing of a positive value on how civility impacted their lives and the lives of those around them, level one of the Model of Influence.

In essence, Mrs. Mathers was attempting to teach her students about social harmony, respect, ideology, and personal philosophy—all higher order thinking principles that are much needed in today's classrooms and beyond. Her awareness of the importance of establishing a classroom environment that fostered the characteristics of good citizenship was shared by Marcus and Jonah.

Through their discussion at lunch, teacher and students *shared perspectives and affirmed their beliefs*, level two of the Model of Influence, not only about citizenship, but also their respective responsibilities in modeling civility with their classmates. This coming together actually led them collectively to *realize benefits to self and others*, level three in the Model of Influence, and ultimately to level four, *taking action and embracing influence*.

FINAL THOUGHTS

In each of the preceding scenarios, teachers were faced with a variety of challenges that can be typically experienced in our schools. Ms. Younger, kindergarten teacher, was challenged by a pending visit from an accrediting agent, distraught children, and other issues that might be experienced in any kindergarten classroom. Mr. Lopez, fifth grade teacher, sought to teach civility to his ever-changing population. His challenges included increasing diversity coupled with a lack of sensitivity and understanding on the part of his students, and possibly his colleagues. Mr. Smithers, eighth grade teacher, was seeking to help his students to refrain from thoughtless, hurtful comments delivered to one another. Finally, Mrs. Mathers, eleventh grade teacher, was seeking to engage her class leaders in promoting consciousness in the valuing of all students.

Although each teacher approached their classrooms in different ways, what connects each of their experiences was the notion of civility, interacting with one another in a positive, considerate way. In each classroom, the teacher sought to *create awareness*, level one in the Model of Influence.

In some cases, the teachers worked with their students to acknowledge and understand their own perspectives as well as *affirm their beliefs*, level two in the model. By the examples shared, you can see that civility goes well beyond being nice; civility preserves our humanity, and it enables us to live and work with one another in an orderly, respectful way.

In the next chapter, Ms. Younger, Mr. Lopez, Mr. Smithers, and Mrs. Mathers will be reintroduced and revisited. The scenarios that were initiated in this chapter will be expanded, but the focus will be on teaching compassion. Each teacher will face new challenges, as he/she uses the Model of Influence as the roadmap for teaching. We will again invite the reader to view each reflectively, and to think about the importance of modeling and teaching a genuine concern for others, compassion.

5

BRINGING COMPASSION TO LIFE

Earlier, in chapters 1 and 3, compassion was defined as having a concern for others, including both a consciousness of another's distress as well as the desire to alleviate the distress. One might ask: To what degree do we empathize with another's perspective or experience? How often do we feel an emotional response to another's distress? Do we desire to help another when he/she is in distress? How do we demonstrate altruistic behaviors?

It is true that we can find and celebrate great humanitarian, compassionate efforts where one or more individuals demonstrate they are deeply moved by the hurt or helplessness of another and equally moved by a deep desire to dissipate that distress. As we step more fully into the twenty-first century, we must help instill in our students this call to consciousness and the stirrings of a powerful desire to reach out. The bombardment of images, stories, and news demonstrating how insensitive people are to one another can be a hindrance, but careful attention to the messages we bring into our classrooms through our teaching, to demonstrate the value of caring for and about other people, can make a powerful difference.

Once again, we ask the reader to become immersed in scenarios designed to provoke thoughts that help *develop consciousness*, the beginning level in the Model of Influence. These stories are illustrative of some of our classroom situations faced by teachers throughout the country. It is our hope that the stories will assist the reader as he/she reflects on the scenario as well as his/her own current classroom condition.

Further, we challenge the reader to examine and acknowledge as well as affirm his/her beliefs, which is the second level from the Model of Influence. The reader will be reintroduced to our characters created in chapter 4: Ms. Younger, kindergarten teacher; Mr. Lopez, fifth grade teacher; Mr. Smithers, eighth grade language arts and social studies teacher; and Mrs. Mathers, eleventh grade science teacher. As in chapter 4, each story is followed by questions for reflection as well as space for thoughts, comments, and other responses to be recorded. We begin again with Ms. Younger.

MS. YOUNGER'S KINDERGARTEN CLASSROOM

"Ms. Younger!" a parent shouts across the parking lot. "I've been wanting to talk with you about a conversation I had with my daughter, a student in your class. Maya came home a couple of days ago and told me about something that happened in class concerning children of military families."

"Maya said that Jacob was crying when the Pledge of Allegiance was recited, and that Jacob said his dad was across the ocean in the Army. Every time Jacob saw the flag, it reminded him of his dad, and he started to cry. Jacob said he doesn't get to talk to his dad because it costs too much money. She told me how sad she was for Jacob and all the other kids who have to be away from their families, and she asked me what she could do so that they wouldn't feel so alone. As you can imagine, I was a bit shocked," she said, *"that a child so young would show such compassion for someone she barely knows."*

The parent goes on to share with Ms. Younger how she conducted a little research and found an organization that helps military families keep in touch by collecting and giving them free cell phones. The parent thinks it might be a great activity for students and families to participate in.

Ms. Younger thinks it is a great idea and a terrific service-learning project for her young students. She begins to plan how her students might create a booth in the front hallway and decorate it so that guests to the building will see it. She thinks she might connect with the math content students are learning by graphing and counting the cell phones that are collected. She also thinks she might introduce some social studies geography concepts related to where family members are around the world. More importantly, she thinks of capitalizing on the reason why those children might feel compelled to collect cell phones and how those phones will benefit the military families.

Think About, Ask, and Reflect

Ms. Younger used a conversation she had with a parent as a catalyst to build on the compassion demonstrated by one of her students, Maya. She could as easily have used other connections, such as her students' experiences with family members, pets, community, or their places of worship.

Ask yourself:

- In what ways did Ms. Younger build awareness among her students from the conversation she had with Maya's mother?
- What perspectives did she seem to have?
- What beliefs did her behaviors portray?
- How are your beliefs and perspectives reflected in your teaching?

Write your thoughts here:

_____
_____
_____
_____
_____
_____
_____

Summing Up Ms. Younger's Class Experience

Although Ms. Younger's inspiration for the cell phone collection project came from one of her student's parents, Ms. Younger was moved to action by her desire to cultivate compassion in her kindergarten class. What was most important was her commitment to *create an awareness* and help her young students begin to *affirm their beliefs*, level one in the Model of Influence, through her careful planning. Ms. Younger connected other content areas as she built upon student expressions of care and concern for others.

MR. LOPEZ'S FIFTH GRADE CLASSROOM

On Monday, Mrs. Dolton, the principal, notifies Mr. Lopez that he will have a new student joining his class in a few weeks. Mrs. Dolton is somewhat concerned because the student has cerebral palsy and she wants to make sure his students are prepared. Mr. Lopez is excited to welcome a new student into his class and understands Mrs. Dolton's concerns, given the incident that happened a few weeks ago between Amira and Samuel.

Mr. Lopez also knows that over the past several weeks his students have learned a great deal about other cultures and customs, and are demonstrating civility one to another. So, he decides to have a conversation about what they can do that might help them create a classroom and a school plan for welcoming new students.

"Class, in a few days we will have a new student. Her name is Holly. Holly has a condition called cerebral palsy. Does anyone know what that is?" No students answer. Mr. Lopez then introduces Holly's mother, Mrs. Garcia, who assists Mr. Lopez in giving the students a brief overview of cerebral palsy. Both Mr. Lopez and Mrs. Garcia stress that Holly is like any other fifth grade student, but that some of her needs are a bit different.

Mr. Lopez then asks them to think about how they felt when they started at a new school. He also asks them to consider what they can do to welcome any new student, how to help them adjust and make friends, and learn how they might create something to help new students find rooms in the school. The students come up with lots of idea of what they can do to welcome any new student into the school and classroom.

After reviewing their ideas, Mr. Lopez says, "We are going to work in small groups to expand our thoughts. Some of you will work on creating a school-wide welcome plan for any student. Others of you will work on how we, as a classroom, can welcome Holly and make her feel comfortable. Then we will meet with Mrs. Dolton and other teachers and present our plan. Mrs. Dolton is interested in adopting the welcome plan and instituting it school-wide."

The students become quite excited about the welcome plan. Mr. Lopez plans ways he will integrate math and social studies, and certainly literacy, into this project. He divides the class into several teams. Two groups work on specific plans for welcoming Holly and any other new students to their class. Other groups begin working on a school-wide plan.

Think About, Ask, and Reflect

While Mr. Lopez certainly wanted his students to have a healthy respect for Holly and welcome her into the classroom, he also saw this as an opportunity to engage them in a much larger project that would benefit far more students and the school.

Ask yourself:

- How did Mr. Lopez cultivate an awareness with his students about the needs of new students?
- How did he build on that awareness?
- What beliefs did he portray?
- In what ways did he engage his students?
- How might you cultivate an awareness of the needs of others in your classroom?

Write your thoughts here:

_____
_____
_____
_____
_____
_____
_____

Summing Up Mr. Lopez's Class Experience

Mr. Lopez connected his students with others by utilizing their prior experiences and asking them to reflect on those experiences in preparing for the arrival of a new student. In so doing, Mr. Lopez was able to teach lessons about showing compassion to others by first acknowledging how they felt as new students in new school. Because of Mr. Lopez's commitment to all his students, he creatively strengthened the level of inclusiveness throughout the school community.

MR. SMITHERS' EIGHTH GRADE CLASSROOM

In Mr. Smithers' eighth grade classroom, several students spend the weekend serving food to homeless veterans at a local shelter through their church. After speaking with the students about their experience, Mr. Smithers asks the students to share their experiences with the class—what they are learning about the shelter, the veterans, and their needs. He thinks this might potentially be a great way to engage his students in a service-learning project to help homeless veterans in an effort to increase students' care and compassion for others in need, as well as, teach several eighth grade learning standards.

The following morning, Mr. Smithers begins class with a brief discussion of information about the number of homeless veterans in the country. He asks the students to come to the front of the class to share their experiences.

"Over the weekend," one student begins, "we spent time at a homeless shelter for veterans. We served meals and talked with them about sports, cars, and other things they like to do." Another student chimes in: "I thought they were going to be mean, but they were actually really nice!" "We talked with the shelter's director," a third student says, "and he told us about their food and clothing truck that serves the ones who don't come to the shelter. He also said that they have a hard time keeping volunteers and are always in the need of clothes, food, and people who can teach basic computer skills."

The students add their thoughts and perspectives to the conversation. Many of the other students ask questions and seem to be quite interested in the veterans' lives. As the conversation comes to a close, Mr. Smithers asks a few reflection questions. "So, what did we learn about homeless veterans and the shelter? What might we do to help them and how could we help the shelter meet the needs of the veterans?"

Mr. Smithers divides the students into small groups with the objective of having groups engage in short research projects on homeless veterans and the many organizations that serve them. He asks them to focus on national and well as local organizations. He asks students to think about three things the class might do together to help support veterans and veteran-support organizations in the community.

Think About, Ask, and Reflect

Mr. Smithers, like so many great teachers, was using his students' interests to engage their academic and social emotional learning through a purposeful project. He began by engaging them in a conversation—a wondering about something that has the potential to teach vital lessons about compassion and caring for others in needs.

Ask yourself:

- How did Mr. Smithers cultivate awareness within his students of the needs of the homeless veterans?
- How did he begin to set a foundation for the development of a consciousness of those around his eighth grade students?
- What were the perspectives and beliefs held by Mr. Smithers?
- How might your beliefs compare with Mr. Smithers' beliefs?
- How can you engage your students in such a way that the development of a compassionate and caring consciousness emerge?

Write your thoughts here:

_____
_____
_____
_____
_____
_____
_____

Summing Up Mr. Smithers' Class Experience

By helping students build an awareness of the needs of homeless veterans, Mr. Smithers was working to set a foundation for the *development of a consciousness*—an understanding of those around you and their perspectives. This is the first level in the Model of Influence. As the project expands, Mr. Smithers planned to engage his students in various lessons to teach traditional academic content and higher-order academic skills as well. In following chapters we will provide example lessons of how one might integrate academic content into such planning and learning.

MRS. MATHERS' ELEVENTH GRADE CLASSROOM

Before making a career change to teaching her, Mrs. Mathers was an alternative energy consultant. As often as possible she tries to integrate her past work with her current work, teaching eleventh grade integrated science. Lately, her students have expressed some interest in how alternative energy works. Mrs. Mathers contacts a local alternative energy company to ask if they would like to partner with her classroom, and possibly the school, on a project to help students learn more about wind, solar, and water powered energy.

While working with her students on researching the origins of alternative energy, she learns of an organization that builds solar power structures for villages in central Africa. Mrs. Mathers sees this as a golden opportunity to teach her students about caring for the environment and other people. She expands her instructional scope to integrate more social studies and math topics into the project while ensuring her students receive an authentic and real-world learning experience.

Mrs. Mathers begins, "Students, we have a great opportunity to use our learning to help other people. So far, we have learned about how alternative energy works and how it can lower cost and help the environment. Well, there are some people in the world who only have electricity for a few hours a day. Sometimes they may not have electricity for days at a time."

Mrs. Mathers then plans a Skype conference with her classroom and one of the project coordinators stationed in Africa to show and tell students exactly what they do. Students are intrigued to learn about the people who live in the village as much as they are about the solar powered structures the organization built.

Over the next several weeks, the students engage in traditional content learning, but also learn how this type of technology impacts their lives and the lives of others around the world. Each week the students use Skype with the coordinator, meet villagers, befriend many of the children, and exchange customs. Mrs. Mathers is pleased to have provided the students with a rich learning experience that allows them to look beyond themselves and see how they can impact the lives of others.

Through the alternative energy project, Mrs. Mathers' students learn that many of the children do not have shoes to wear on their long walk from home to school. This leads to another project where the students engage in research, economics, logistics, and other higher-order thinking topics to raise funds to purchase shoes through a local shoe store with a philanthropic arm and organize shoe drives to collect new or used shoes to send to the village.

BRINGING COMPASSION TO LIFE

Think About, Ask, and Reflect

With her instruction, Mrs. Mathers' students practiced several higher-order and critical thinking skills. Her lessons on alternative energy sources led to a project designed to help children across the world get needed clothing and shoes.

Ask yourself:

- In what ways did Mrs. Mathers use the content to help her students develop care and compassion for other people as well as their environment?
- How did Mrs. Mathers integrate the traditional as well as social-emotional competencies without compromising students' learning expectations and performance?
- What perspectives and beliefs did Mrs. Mathers most likely hold?
- How might you create awareness of issues, problems, or situations by using student interest?
- What beliefs do you hold that might be used to create student awareness?
- How do your teaching practices support the development of compassion in your students?

Write your thoughts here:

_____
_____
_____
_____
_____
_____
_____

Summing Up Mrs. Mathers' Class Experience

One might ask, "How is the Model of Influence reflected in this scenario?" Mrs. Mathers used her students' interest to build a curriculum that allowed them to become more aware of an issue, problem, or situation.

They then began to engage in activities and instruction which afforded them an opportunity to learn about the subject at a deeper level. Third, they certainly began to see how alternative energy was valuable to them and others. The project led to other learning opportunities where students acknowledged and embraced their influence to positively change the lives of others.

FINAL THOUGHTS

In the preceding scenarios, our four teachers, Ms. Younger, Mr. Lopez, Mr. Smithers, and Mrs. Mathers each followed a different approach to creating an awareness of the importance of compassion in their respective classes. In Ms. Smithers' class, one of her students was distraught by another student's sadness about his absent father; in Mr. Lopez's class, the promise of a new student served as the impetus for developing and refining a school-wide process; for Mr. Smithers, creating an awareness for compassionate behavior grew out of volunteer activities some of his students engaged in during the weekend; and for Mrs. Mathers' science class, an alternative energy project grew into a powerful connection with individuals across the world.

Perhaps now, more than any other time in history, compassion is critically needed. Our world cries out for those who would reach out to another with the willingness to share experiences and empathize with another's distress. Daily, we are presented with images of horrific acts and occurrences throughout the world. The onslaught of inhumanity and unkindness, carelessness and intentional acts of cruelty pervade our culture. Children grow up witnessing violence and mayhem. How, then can we combat what is impossible to ignore?

A simple saying comes to mind: life is the act of planting seeds. The image of the seed, growing in the dark, wet ground while reaching upward and forward into the light, a seed that, given nurturing nutrients—sunlight, warmth, and care—lives to bear fruit and nourish the world. Compassion, when given to another, is as the sower scattering the seeds. Only by promoting acts of compassion can we turn the tide of history.

In chapter 6 we will follow Ms. Younger, Mr. Lopez, Mr. Smithers, and Mrs. Mathers one last time. Our scenarios will reach a culmination, as each teacher seeks to create awareness of the importance of courage. Our scenarios will once again expand as we invite our readers to think about how these teachers work within their classrooms to follow the path created by the Model of Influence.

6

BRINGING COURAGE TO LIFE

Having the inner strength to do something which frightens you is how courage was defined in chapters 1 and 3. Mighty words such as boldness, bravery, fortitude, valor, and grit have been used to describe this often revered trait. At times, it seems we all give lip service to the promotion of tenacity, guts, and spirit until the expression of those traits seems to come up against our own firmly held beliefs.

We contend that courage takes many forms, and that the potential results from having taken a tentative, perhaps even fearful step forward, can have positive ramifications that might potentially change the world. As teachers, we must ask ourselves: how do we encourage our students to boldly step forward? In what ways do we provide a safe environment that encourages the most timid of students to self-advocate or even advocate for another? How do we promote questioning from our students, even when the values they express are different from our own?

Pignatelli suggests that courage means "to be morally accountable to one's self, colleagues, and students and their families" and that it requires modesty and persistence (Pignatelli, 2010). Perhaps the best gift we can give our students is the gift of moral accountability as we promote their tentative, sometimes hesitant steps forward in giving voice to what takes amazing mettle and nerve to share.

The reader is encouraged to contemplate the following stories and to reflect upon the various ways these incredible teachers sought to promote courage within their classrooms. Once again we offer a challenge to our readers, asking them to note how the first and second steps from our Model of Influence: *developing consciousness and acknowledging and affirming beliefs* resonate.

We believe that the stories as well as the questions for reflection will serve the reader as he/she turns within through introspection and examines his or her own teaching practice. As with previous chapters, there is space provided for the recording of the reader's thoughts and comments.

MS. YOUNGER'S KINDERGARTEN CLASSROOM

Ms. Peterson, teaching assistant, walks in the classroom to find Ms. Younger in tears. "Clarice? What's wrong?" she says, rushing to her side. "Well, I overheard a couple of teachers talking in the hallway about one of our families in the most awful way."

Ms. Younger proceeds to tell Ms. Peterson about these two teachers who laughed and scoffed in disgust at the family and their children's appearance. It is well known and obvious that this family has fallen on difficult times. The dad has lost his job. The family has lost their apartment and are now living with other family members or friends when they can, but frequently find shelter in their older car.

The daughter, Kimber, who is in Ms. Younger's classroom, and the son, Thomas, who is in one of the scoffing teacher's classrooms, comes to school in dirty and sometimes smelly clothes with disheveled hair—clearly this family is in an awful predicament.

After hearing the story, Ms. Peterson says, "We have to do something! How insensitive to speak of this family in that way!" Ms. Younger and Ms. Peterson decide they will advocate for the family by working with the school counselor to create a "Living Well" space for families in the parent center with information, personal hygiene items, children's clothing, and so on.

They also decide to launch a campaign to support teachers in demonstrating compassion and showing empathy toward their families in need. Most courageously, these teachers decide to stand up to the other teachers who ridiculed the students and their family and help them, their colleagues, find more caring and productive ways of communicating about families.

Think About, Ask, and Reflect

As the reader can clearly see, this scenario is not about strategies a teacher incorporated in her lesson to promote the development of civility, courage, or compassion in her classroom. Instead, the actions only reflect adult behavior. By thinking about the teachers and their response to their colleagues, we can see that Ms. Peterson and Ms. Younger had several choices: they could have been bystanders, listening to the overheard conversation while choosing not to respond.

Perhaps the homeless students their colleagues were referencing were students from another grade or even another wing of the school. Ms. Peterson and Ms. Younger might have wanted to ensure their lack of involvement because it might have resulted in additional conversation or work.

We know from chapter 4 that Ms. Younger was under pressure with the licensing board visit. She was also seeking ways to deliver content to her eager learners.

Ask yourself:

- Why did Ms. Younger need to engage in any action in response to her colleagues' comments?
- What perspectives and beliefs did Ms. Younger and Ms. Peterson hold?
- What do you do in similar situations?
- How do you respond when overworked, overtired, and ready for the end of the day, and you overhear a lack of compassion or even civility from a colleague?
- How does "moral accountability" figure into your behavior?
- What would you do?

Write your thoughts here:

_____
_____
_____
_____
_____
_____
_____

Summing Up Ms. Younger's Class Experience

Courage, sometimes more than any other attribute, takes conscious effort and grit. In the case of Ms. Peterson and Ms. Younger, their choices including standing by as bystanders or moving forward as action-takers. In this instance, they took bold action. Rather than sit on the sidelines, they stepped into the ring. Being morally accountable for their students and their families led these women to creatively address a need exhibited by those served by their school and to confront unkind behavior exhibited by their colleagues.

MR. LOPEZ' FIFTH GRADE CLASSROOM

"Mr. Lopez," Samantha says, *"I was talking with a couple of other kids and we don't think there are enough activities that Holly can do during gym class, and she's left out a lot. We don't think that's fair!"*

"Wow, Sam, how courageous was that for you all to stand up for Holly. Have you talked with Holly about things she likes to do or would like to do during gym class?"

"Well, kind of. Holly had a sleepover with some of the other girls in our class last week, and she told us that she hated gym because it made her feel stupid. She likes to race. She said at her last school, she would race other kids in her wheelchair. But, when we mentioned it to Mr. Thompson, he didn't think it was safe. Holly even asked Mr. Thompson for something else to do. He told Holly he couldn't see how she could participate in the floor activities the other students were engaged in. So Holly just has to sit and watch other kids play. What can we do?"

Mr. Lopez thinks about it for a while and said, *"Samantha, how about you and Holly get together with the other concerned kids and find out what kinds of things Holly would like to do. Make a list of the benefits and challenges of these activities for Holly or any student in a wheelchair. You might conduct an Internet search for organizations that support students with disabilities and see if they have any suggestions or recommendations. Then we can talk with her family, the occupational therapist, and Mr. Thompson to see how we might modify some of the activities so that Holly has more opportunities to participate during gym."*

He asks Holly, who was right there next to Samantha, what she thinks about the ideas. Holly agrees, and says she has some great ideas about websites to look at. She had done some research with her mom and her teachers at her previous school to expand her options in gym.

Mr. Lopez is really proud of his students for advocating for another student's needs. He thinks it demonstrates compassion for each other, but it was also quite courageous of them to see a problem and take action to solve that problem. In this scenario these students clearly have developed a consciousness of Holly's condition and how that affects her. But they also understand Holly's desire to participate more during certain activities.

Think About, Ask, and Reflect

As Holly has become a part of Mr. Lopez's fifth grade class, the other students have become her friends and embraced her, recognizing that Holly is just another fifth grade student with her own unique attributes and qualities. Her needs, while in some ways are different, are basically the same as the other members of the class.

Mr. Lopez has helped his students to develop awareness and create a consciousness that has led them to speak out and up for the needs of a classmate. In addition, Holly is beginning to exhibit personal courage by speaking up for her needs and collaborating with her new friends to be solution focused.

Ask yourself:

- How was this awareness and consciousness created among the fifth grade students?
- What perspectives and beliefs were manifested in Mr. Lopez's behavior and interactions with his students?
- In looking at your beliefs, how might they compare to those held by Mr. Lopez?
- Lastly, what might you do to cultivate compassion that leads to courageous action?

Write your thoughts here:

_____
_____
_____
_____
_____
_____
_____

Summing Up Mr. Lopez's Class Experience

Mr. Lopez provided a safe environment that supported his students when they noticed the needs of others. Through their compassion, his students were moved to step out with courage. By having students engage in developing activities with Holly for use in her gym class, there was a potential benefit to her and others, including faculty members. Most importantly, these students, with the help of their teacher, are taking action to influence the lives of others around them.

MR. SMITHERS' EIGHTH GRADE CLASSROOM

Mr. Smithers' class is very excited to start working on their anti-bullying PSAs. Groups are formed, and most students appear to be working well together. As they delve deeper into their planning and preparation phase, some of the group's cohesion begins to break down. Students become frustrated with their group members and begin struggling to meet the benchmarks and requirements outlined on the assignment rubric.

As a result of their earlier work on civility, negativity toward one another is not evident. What Mr. Smithers notices is students pulling away from the assignment, muttering that they can't do it, refusing to seek guidance. Mr. Smithers realizes the groups need help, but he does not just want to provide them with information and suggestions for the project. He wants to make this into a lesson about courage and facing adversity. He understands that students are afraid to ask for help for fear of being perceived unintelligent or seemingly unable to complete their assignments, especially when so many other groups appear to be working fine.

Mr. Smithers begins, "Let's talk about your projects and do a little bit of troubleshooting. I've noticed that some of you are struggling with a few elements, and you seem to be frustrated."

Mr. Smithers goes on to explain how courage might apply in this situation and offers some strategies individual and groups of students might use to advocate for themselves and others as they work together to complete their assignment. He asks students to define what courage means to them and how that definition applies to the project. Mr. Smithers deepens his students' understanding by asking them to reflect on how avoidance and helplessness might negatively impact their work and performance on future assignments and in life.

"So, for the next 15 minutes, I want groups to get together and create a list of questions or concerns they have and strategies the team can imple-

ment to resolve those issues," Mr. Smithers directs. As groups organize themselves and their thoughts, Mr. Smithers spends a few minutes with each group answering a few questions. However, what he notices is that most groups have a renewed sense of purpose, and the palpable frustration seems lessened, especially for those groups that seem to struggle more than others.

Think About, Ask, and Reflect

In this scenario, Mr. Smithers did not necessarily plan to teach a lesson on courage, but recognized that his students were struggling with their confidence and perseverance and decided to provide them with a lesson on facing adversity to achieve success. Often times it's an empowering message to students that can serve as the best lesson.

Ask yourself:

- How did Mr. Smithers provide a safe environment that encouraged his students to speak up?
- How did Mr. Smithers promote self-advocacy?
- How did his discussion about courage impact his students' behaviors?
- What were Mr. Smithers' perspectives and beliefs regarding courage?
- In situations when your students withdraw and turn inward with negative self-directed messages, how do you respond?
- What beliefs do you have concerning the promotion of courage as defined by promoting sometimes hesitant steps forward?

Write your thoughts here:

_____
_____
_____
_____
_____
_____

Summing Up Mr. Smithers' Class Experience

Courage is an attribute that often involves many other affirmations such as bravery, confidence, and empowerment. Students struggling with avoidance, helplessness, and fear of failure can be paralyzed and unable to achieve or performance an acceptable level. Mr. Smithers understood the need to increase his students' awareness of this attribute to support other efforts of achievement.

MRS. MATHERS' ELEVENTH GRADE CLASSROOM

Mrs. Mathers has worked tirelessly with her students on establishing positive relationships with one another as well as fostering a climate of caring and compassion between her students and the students in Africa with whom they were communicating. The work that is getting accomplished on behalf of the children who have no shoes is astounding to Mrs. Mathers as well as her students. What happens next, then, comes as a complete surprise.

On an early Monday morning, Mrs. Mathers is summoned to the principal's office, where she is told that an anonymous letter has been written to the city's newspaper, questioning the use of school time to Skype with students from across the world, when the intent of the science class is to teach the science standards. Further, the article asserts, there are plenty of local issues that need to be addressed, if the students are so inclined. They need not concern themselves with children halfway across the world. The article calls for Mrs. Mathers to cease her global activities and to teach in a manner consistent with more traditional schooling.

Although the principal sympathizes with Mrs. Mathers, he does not want the wrath of the community to come down around him. He informs Mrs. Mathers that there will be a district meeting during which she can defend herself.

Mrs. Mathers takes the concern to her class and informs them of the letter. One of her students, Emily, tearfully raises her hand and shares with the class that her dad is the one who wrote the letter. Emily had begged him not to, but her dad was insistent that the letter be written and sent.

As one student stands up, and points a finger at Emily, telling her that her dad ruined class for them all, Mrs. Mathers gently states that Emily's revelation takes tremendous courage. Quieted, the students ask Mrs. Mathers what can be done. Mrs. Mathers then asks them what they want to do.

Emily speaks again, suggesting that the students work to prepare a presentation to be delivered by them at the district meeting, sharing the work they have accomplished while working toward mastery of the science standards. As the students are planning to develop their presentation, Mrs. Mathers shares other stories and examples of courage from the work of Ghandi, King, Kennedy, and others. Then, her students get to work on their presentation.

Think About, Ask, and Reflect

Mrs. Mathers affirmed that her students had shown great courage: Emily for standing up and sharing what had happened at home with the class, and her classmates for deciding to stand up and defend and explain their work at the district meeting, not knowing the outcome, and facing scrutiny of the district's leaders.

Ask yourself:

- In what ways has Mrs. Mathers provided an environment that lends itself to the expressions of compassion and promotes the courageous stances taken by her students?
- What awareness did she create?
- What attributes has she cultivated?
- What results is she seeing?
- What are the potential benefits resulting from her expression of her beliefs about others?
- In what ways are your beliefs and perspectives reflected in the behaviors of your students?
- How are the results you are seeing mirroring what you believe about compassion? About courage?

Write your thoughts here:

_____
_____
_____
_____
_____
_____

Summing Up Mrs. Mathers' Class Experience

Through her attention and planning over the course of the year, Mrs. Mathers has encouraged her students to advocate for themselves and for the needs of others. She has given them a safe place to share their thoughts and express their feelings. Her perspectives and beliefs have resulted in action. Mrs. Mathers is inspiring her students to take tentative, and yes, bold steps, under her guidance to be morally accountable to their own beliefs. This gift has the potential to change their communities and their world.

FINAL THOUGHTS

Courage, like civility and compassion is essential to one's humanity and reaches beyond the classroom into everyday life experiences. As we move through different levels of influence, it is critical that students expand their understanding—consciousness about concepts, affirm their perspectives and reflect on what learning, organize their thoughts, and place a value on the information received, use this information and learning to benefit self and others, and finally, take action and embrace the influence they have on the lives of others.

The stories were written to be thought provoking, and to urge the reader to examine her own beliefs and actions. They are reflective of a variety of situations in which we find ourselves as teachers. Each one of our fictitious teachers has been confronted with numerous incidents and challenges that have resulted in a call to dig deeply into their innermost thoughts and beliefs about what is, perhaps, most important.

Ms. Younger witnessed unkindness from her colleague, and she had to decide how to respond. Mr. Lopez made the choice to assist his students in the confrontation of a practice that was inequitable. Mr. Smithers supported his students in their struggles with confidence and perseverance. Finally, Mrs. Mathers used the work of historical figures to assist her students in expressing their beliefs about their relationship with others from the larger global community.

These teachers have had to contemplate the consequences of remaining on the side, and encouraging their students to remain on the side, as bystanders or to take an uncertain step, even with the outcome unknown, to respond to that fire within that says, "I need to be morally accountable to myself and those around me."

In the following chapters, we will provide a series of sample lessons designed to assist the teacher who seeks to embed civility, compassion, and courage into his or her lesson plans. While the scenarios presented have been reflective of incidental as well as more purposeful teaching, we assert that in order to ensure that our students have *developed an awareness, acknowledged their perspectives,* and *affirmed their beliefs*, we must be intentional in our approach. These lessons are designed to help our students *realize the benefits to themselves and others*, level three of the Model of Influence, and most important, as seen in most of the scenarios, *take action and embrace influence*, the final level.

For each grade level, we provide three sample lessons. Our format includes materials, resources, ideas for extensions, as well as home and community connections. We continue to invite our readers to seek and find ways to insert the three C's: civility, compassion, and courage into every aspect of their teaching process.

REFERENCE

Pignatelli, F. (2010). Everyday courage in the midst of standardization in schools. *Studies in Education* 7(2), 230–235.

7

LESSON PLANS IN CIVILITY

For the next three chapters, we have provided a series of sample lessons to be considered, used, adapted, and made to fit our readers' individual situations. We have written these lessons, keeping in mind several factors. We wanted them to be simple to follow. Each lesson follows a similar format. The lessons begin with the overall lesson goal, then include the specific lesson objective. We have included the focus level for each lesson, based on the Model of Influence.

Each lesson contains a brief instructional set, step-by-step procedures, a list of suggested materials, supplies and resources, ideas for level extensions (if appropriate), home and community connections, and grade modifications (for grades K–2 and 3–5). Where students are asked to develop action plans or other similar processes, we have provided suggested formats which are attached to the lessons or included in the appendices of the book, as appropriate.

Our lessons also include space for the reader/practitioner to add his or her own comments about possible adaptations or modifications to the lesson. We have posed questions for reflection about the lessons' processes and content. In addition, we have embedded questions or comments that may guide the teacher/practitioner to delve more deeply at certain points in the lesson.

Our intent was to write the lessons specific to each characteristic: civility, compassion, and courage, yet we recognize and acknowledge that each lesson can be adapted slightly to allow for its focus to move from one characteristic to another. For instance, we suggest that K–2 students respond to various scenarios that illustrate the concept of civility. With a few adaptations, this lesson could easily apply to compassion or even courage. We were deliberate in this endeavor. Another example is the middle school lesson on civility. The objective for that lesson is to have students craft a personal position statement on civility. Again, students could just as easily be asked to develop a personal position statement on compassion or even courage, with a few adaptations to the lesson as it is currently written. Our most important goal for the writing of the lessons is to give practitioners a variety of ideas for infusing their instruction with careful attention to these characteristics.

Another point we would like to make is that the lessons are designed to fit in any curriculum. Some could easily take place over a period of time, say several weeks. Others can be completed in a much shorter timeframe. Whether in class-building or team-building time for younger students or an activity period or even a student organization for older students, they can serve as a tremendous catalyst for infusing our instruction with these critical concepts. We suggest that teachers, counselors, community partners, and others, as appropriate, be involved in the instruction. What is most important is that they get used!

Finally, we recognize that the lessons do not always necessarily perfectly fit within the grade levels to which they have been assigned. We suggest and even encourage the reader to read through all the lessons on civility. Perhaps there are elements of the middle school lesson that the reader may wish to incorporate in a high school lesson. For some, concepts and content introduced in a lesson for younger students may serve as a foundation for a lesson for older students. Additionally, at the end of the chapter are final thoughts and reflections. We encourage the reader to think about the questions posed and reflect on how these lessons and information shared can be most impactful to the classroom and school's curriculum. We sincerely hope that teachers, administrators, and all others who come in contact with students will notice the positive influence brought about by careful attention to the teaching of the first characteristic, civility.

CIVILITY LESSON PLAN: K–2

Goal: Help students understand what it means to be **CIVIL** in and out of the classroom.
Objective: Define civility, engage in discussion about civility, and demonstrate civility in the classroom, as appropriate.
Focus Level: 1 and 2 (Developing Consciousness and Acknowledging and Affirming Beliefs)
Note: This lesson plan can be implemented over a few days.

Table 7.1.

Lesson Content
Assessments: Development of classroom rules or a behavior contract for students when working in small groups and/or the whole class that represents civil speech, actions, and thinking.

Procedures:	Materials, Supplies, and Resources:
Instructional set • Explain the lesson will introduce a new vocabulary word that will help them learn how to be kind and use kind words. Tell students that they will work in groups to create a group or classroom "behavior contract." Content • Open a discussion about what students think civility means. Give examples of synonyms to help them make connections. • Give examples of what civility looks and feels like. Give examples of incivility for comparison. Note: Consider showing a video or pictures that represent both. • Have a prepared word list and/or phrases that represents civil and incivility. Include more that represent civility. Ask students to identify all of the words or phrases that represent civility. This could be done with partners or a whole group. Use a t-chart to organize words and phrases. Students report out. • Ask students how civility can be demonstrated in the classroom. Give students various scenarios to respond to. For example, ask students how they would feel if someone said . . . or what they would do if someone. . . . Ask them to explain why they choose that response or how that action demonstrates civility. • Have students work in groups of four to develop and write two things they could do to show civility toward each other. Tell students their ideas will be a part of a behavior contract that	• Chart paper or handout with synonyms and phrases for civility. *Note: Create posters to put in the classroom or make copies for groups to have at their tables as reminders. Use contact paper to protect the table copies from damage. Use the posters as a **behavior set**—a reminder for students who need redirection or it can be used at the beginning of any lesson to remind students of the type of behaviors they are expected to demonstrate.*

Table 7.1. *(continued)*

Procedures:	Materials, Supplies, and Resources:
everyone, including the teacher, will use to show civility and that everyone will be expected to help remind those who forget. • Explain what a behavior contract is. *Note: Instead of a behavior contract, you might create class rules, or a class motto using the students' ideas—creating ownership.* • Help them craft those ideas into a behavior contract. Use positive language. *For example, I will listen when others are talking and not interrupt. Exp: I will help my group keep our table clean.* Closing • Review the definition and why civility is important in and out of the classroom. Explain that the behavior contract will be a reminder of how we agreed to interact with one another and behave appropriately.	**For Teachers:** **How would you modify this lesson to meet the needs of your students? Alternative materials, resources?** *Note: A more hands-on approach might be to give partners or triads an envelope and have them discuss and sort the words into categories.*

Table 7.2.

Level Extensions:	None for this lesson.
Home and Community Connections:	• Send information home with parents explaining what students are doing in class. Ask parents to work with their child on how this behavior contract can be translated at home. Have students present their ideas during a future class.
Kindergarten • Draw a picture that represents civility in the classroom. Have students write a sentence that describes the picture, if they can or have students present their pictures to the class.	Second Grade • Create their own posters. This could be individually, partners, or groups. • Give groups or partners various scenarios to act out. • Use a KWL chart throughout the lesson.

LESSON PLANS IN CIVILITY

CIVILITY LESSON PLAN: 3–5

Goal: Help students understand the concept of **CIVILITY** and what it means to be **CIVIL** in and out of the classroom.
  Objective: Demonstrate civility in the classroom, as appropriate.
  Focus Level: 3 and 4 (Benefit to Self and Others and Taking Action and Embracing Influence)
  Note: This example lesson is one that should be impelled as a service-learning project or project-based learning assignment.

Table 7.3.

Lesson Content	
Assessments: Students will create a pro-civility video where students role play various types of civil acts, speech, and behaviors in the classroom and school.	
Procedures:	**Materials, Supplies, and Resources:**
Instructional set • Explain that the lesson will introduce a new vocabulary word that will help learn them how to be kind and use kind words; how to show civility in the classroom and outside of the classroom. Tell students that they will work in groups to create a pro-civility video. *Note: Consider making this video a part of a larger anti-bullying or **pro-civility** campaign in the school or within a grade level.* Content (step-by-step procedures) • Open a discussion about what students think civility means. Give examples of synonyms to help them make connections. • Give examples of what civility looks and feels like. Give example of incivility for comparison. • Discuss how those actions can translate into bullying or inappropriate actions and behaviors. • Show clips from the movie *The Bully* (2012) or the full feature. Another option might be *The Cyber Bullying Full Movie*.	• *Bullying* (movie, 2012) Director: Lee Hirsch • *CyberBully* (movie, 2011) Director: Charles Binamé. ABC Family • *The Cyber Bullying Full Movie* (2014) Director: Jimmie Harris http://vimeo.com/89102621 • Discussion questions • Rubrics, assignment descriptions/instructions

Table 7.3. (*continued*)

Procedures:	Materials, Supplies, and Resources:
Note: There are several other short films on YouTube that might be used in place of these full-length feature movies. • Discuss students' feelings before, during, and after the movie. • Discuss the pro-civility project. Divide students into groups. Provide them with guidelines, rubrics, and instructions. Assign group jobs so that everyone has some accountability to the project. For example, director, camera person, editor, writer. Give students class time to divide up the responsibilities and develop some preliminary ideas for their videos. *Note: Consider working with the I/T person in your school or computer teacher on the video production. Also consider making this into a more extensive project that covers more depth, information, and time. Find ways to integrate other content areas, such as social studies and literacy.* <u>Closing</u> • Review the definition and why civility is important in and out of the classroom. Provide students with next steps for their projects.	**For Teachers:** **How would you modify this lesson to meet the needs of your students? Alternative materials, resources?**

Table 7.4.

Level Extensions:	This lesson is written with the assumption that students have a developed consciousness and affirmed beliefs about civility.
Home and Community Connections:	If this is a larger service-learning project, for instance, partner with local and/or national anti-bullying organizations and programs to showcase students' work. Here are a few national organizations: Pacer's National Bullying Prevention; Center; End to Cyber Bullying Organization; The Bully Project; GLSEN (Gay, Lesbian, Straight, Education Network)
Grade Modifications	
Third • Create a list of words that demonstrate civility. Have students create a wordle. • If possible, partner with a local t-shirt company to create t-shirts as a fundraiser. Give the monies raised to a local anti-bullying organization.	Fourth • Write a story that represents how someone might demonstrate civility. • Integrate social studies and literacy and have students research historical figures who have demonstrated civility.

CIVILITY LESSON PLAN: GRADES 6–8

Goal: Help students move from an awareness of the meaning of **CIVILITY** to engage in rich dialog that promotes the deep examination of one's own beliefs.

Objective: Develop personal position statement regarding civility.

Focus Level: 1 and 2 (Developing Consciousness and Acknowledging and Affirming Beliefs)

Note: Although students in the middle grades are assumed to know what civility means, and can identify civil as well as uncivil behaviors, many students have not engaged in contemplation nor have they developed an active approach to the true meaning and impact of what is meant by embracing civility as a quality to be cultivated and promoted.

Table 7.5.

Lesson Content
Assessments: Students will articulate their personal position statement on the characteristic civility. Articulation may be in written, spoken, illustrated, or other form. Students will explain their personal statement to peers, teacher(s), and others as deemed appropriate.

Procedures:	Materials, Supplies, and Resources:
Instructional set • Inform students that the purpose of the lesson is to have them develop a personal position statement on what it means to be civil Content • Using any recent set of events, either local or global, that illustrate civility as well as incivility, ask students to comment on what they see and hear. • Capture their impressions on the board or other means of visual display. • Next, ask students to use words to describe how the images/story/video etc. made them feel. • Record their descriptions of their feelings • Using a Venn diagram or other visual representation, such as a graphic organizer, compare the two images/stories/videos, asking how are they alike and how are they different. • Ask students to reflect quietly for a minute or two on their own behaviors toward others. Ask questions such as what behaviors do you exhibit that demonstrate respect? How important is it to be polite? What words do you use that could be viewed as polite and courteous? What words do you use that might be heard as impolite or courteous? • Ask students to share their thoughts with the class or with a partner or small group, emphasizing that individual shared responses are to be listened to. Questions can be asked for clarification, but commenting on the rightness or wrongness of another student's response is not to take place.	• Newspaper • Youtube videos • Recent news stories (choose from any or all media sources) Format and examples for writing personal position statements: • http://www.wamcstudenttownmeetings.org/pdf/instructional-materials/writing-a-personal-position-statement.pdf_ • http://education-portal.com/academy/lesson/position-statement-definition-examples-quiz.html#lesson *Note: There are many kinds of graphic organizers available for comparing and contrasting two or more concepts or ideas. The use of them provides a visual representation of information for students who process better visually.* **For Teachers:** **How would you modify this lesson to meet the needs of your students? Alternative materials, resources?**

Procedures:	Materials, Supplies, and Resources:
• After students have had an opportunity to reflect and respond, define personal position statement as a statement of how they feel about civility. • Ask students to draft a personal position statement about civility. A sample format (and other information) for drafting a personal position statement is identified under the materials and resources column. • Invite students to share with the class or a small group. • Next, ask students to think about their position statement and to reflect on the behaviors they currently exhibit regarding civility, giving themselves a rating of 1–10 on how close their behaviors match their statement (this may be a private rating or a public rating depending on student preference). <u>Closing</u> • Review the lesson's purpose, and ask students to comment on the process of developing a personal position statement. Ask them to share their statement with their parents or other significant individuals and to think about any revisions they might want to make to their statements. Suggest that students think about a place to keep their statement for quick reference.	*Note: Refer to the list of materials and resources for a personal position statement format.*
Level Extensions: (ideas for applications for next three levels)	*Note: A sample action plan format is included at the end of the chapter. These extensions can be adapted to meet a variety of student needs. What is most important is that the discussion and attention to students' action plans continue.*
Level 2 (Acknowledging Perspectives and Affirming Beliefs)	• Ask students to develop an action plan that identifies steps, if any, they will take to merge their behaviors with their position statement on civility. A simple action plan answers these questions: What needs to be done? When does it need to be done? How will I know I have met this step?

Table 7.5. (continued)

Level Extensions: (ideas for applications for next three levels)	*Note: A sample action plan format is included at the end of the chapter. These extensions can be adapted to meet a variety of student needs. What is most important is that the discussion and attention to students' action plans continue.*
Level 2 (Acknowledging Perspectives and Affirming Beliefs)	• Ask students to develop an action plan that identifies steps, if any, they will take to merge their behaviors with their position statement on civility. A simple action plan answers these questions: What needs to be done? When does it need to be done? How will I know I have met this step?
Level 3 (Realizing Benefits to Self and Others)	• Using the action plan that students have written (see Level 2 Extension), ask them to keep a record of the progress they have made toward meeting the expectations that were set forth in the plan. • Engage students in periodic discussion about the benefits of working toward their stated goals. Ask them to revise their steps as needed.
Level 4 (Taking Action and Embracing Influence)	• Using the action plan that students have written (see Level 2 Extension), ask students to keep a journal recording instances when they exhibited civil behavior toward others, detailing the effects on both themselves and others.
Home and Community Connections: (possible organizations, ideas to do with parents, ways it is demonstrated outside of school)	• Have students work with younger students, through their church, feeder school, or other venue, sharing ways to demonstrate civility to others. Discuss being role models for others, and the responsibilities of serving as a mentor/role model.

CIVILITY LESSON PLAN: GRADES 9–12

Goal: Assist students to understand the effect that their **CIVIL** behaviors have on the individuals and the world around them, and to help them make purposeful decisions that will result in having a positive impact on others.

Objective: Develop and implement a plan of action that promotes courteous, polite, and respectful behaviors.

Focus Level: 3 and 4 (Realizing Benefits to Self and Others and Taking Action and Embracing Influence)

Note: The content in this "lesson" is designed to be covered, discussed, and processed over a period of time that extends beyond one or two class periods. The content of the presented lesson is a suggested way to get started.

Table 7.6.

Lesson Content
Assessments: Students will develop an action plan that includes identification of ways they will know that they have been successful in their implementation of the plan. In addition to identifying impact on others, students will determine how they will know that there has been a personal impact.

Procedures:	Materials, Supplies, and Resources:
Instructional set • Tell students that the purpose of the lesson(s) is to explore the relevance of our lives to others and to take action in an effort to make a positive impact on the lives of others	Definition of Chaos Theory: • http://encyclopedia.kids.net.au/page/dy/Dynamical_systems_and_chaos_theory Technology Applications: • See list at end of lesson for helpful websites.
Content • Introduce the lesson by using the example of a pebble dropped into still water. Ask students what happens to the water when the pebble is dropped (the ripple left by the disturbance goes on endlessly). • You may wish to introduce the terms "butterfly effect" and "chaos theory." • Engage student in a discussion about their beliefs concerning whether a small thing has or can have a major effect. • Shift the conversation to the effects that their behaviors have on others, in particular, when they are courteous, polite, respectful, and/or appreciative of others' contributions.	Action Plan Template: • Template is attached at end of chapter. Student journals *Note: For simplicity's sake, the butterfly effect is the concept of small things having major effects. A relatively simple definition can be found on the website listed under resources. In many theoretical instances, the resulting effect is a catastrophic change.*

Table 7.6. (*continued*)

Procedures:	Materials, Supplies, and Resources:
• Ask students to share their experiences, either from the perspective as initiator (the effect their behaviors have on others) or from the perspective of recipient (the effect others' behaviors have on them). • Ask students about the effects they wish to have on others. You may want to discuss the term "legacy," defined as something handed down to others. • As students process, you may wish to have them write a statement about the legacy they wish to leave or the effects they wish their actions to have on others. • Following this part of the lesson, ask students to increase their awareness of the impact they have on others by journaling or keeping record of evidence. • Students can submit evidence through a blog, Dropbox folder, or other means of sharing. • Engage students in a discussion about creating opportunities to take purposeful action within their lives, family, church, or community to promote civil behaviors. • Collectively or in small teams, work with students to identify places where they wish to have a positive effect on others. It may be beneficial to work as a class initially, then work as teams or individuals on subsequent projects. • Using a simple template, have students identify the following information: Name of Project, Statement of Need (why they chose this), Outcome (what they wish to have happen), Getting Started (their initial proposed actions), Next Steps (sustaining their action), and Impact (actual results). Work with students to identify ways they will know that they have been successful. In addition to identifying impact on others, ask students to determine how they will	**For Teachers:** **How would you modify this lesson to meet the needs of your students? Alternative materials, resources?** *Note: A list of resources for developing a blog and other means of sharing information through technology is provided in the appendix. Dropbox can be accessed through www.dropbox.com.* *Note: This action plan template is provided at end of chapter.*

LESSON PLANS IN CIVILITY

	Materials, Supplies, and Resources:
know that there has been an impact on themselves. • Consider having a time and place for students to share what they have worked on. Use a poster display, PowerPoint, or Prezi presentation or other means of sharing. Closing As the projects draw to a close, engage students in discussion about sustaining their work. Devote regular time to the sharing of updates and other opportunities seized upon.	*Note: Information on creating a Prezi and PowerPoint is located in the appendix.*

Table 7.7.

Level Extensions: (ideas for applications for next three levels)	*Note: This lesson series is designed to begin at Level 3 (Realizing Benefits to Self and Others) and to extend into Level 4 (Taking Action and Embracing Influence). It is assumed that most students in grades 9–12 will be ready to participate fully in the ideas presented. If students do not seem to be ready, the reader is referred to the lesson plan designed for middle school (grades 6–8) presented earlier in this chapter.*
Home and Community Connections: (possible organizations, ideas to do with parents, ways it is demonstrated outside of school) • Typically, there are numerous community organizations that can provide opportunities for engaging in civility-focused projects. Several organizations and their website addresses are listed on the right.	Helpful websites: • http://www.character.org/wp-content/uploads/creating-extraordinary-citizens/Who-Is-Welcome-Here-Activities-for-Schools-in-the-Civility-Project.pdf • http://publiclibrariesonline.org/2013/04/choose-civility-public-libraries-take-center-stage/ • http://fundforcivility.org/antibullying/ • http://www.doorcountycivilityproject.org/in-the-news---door-county-civility.html

Table 7.7. *(continued)*

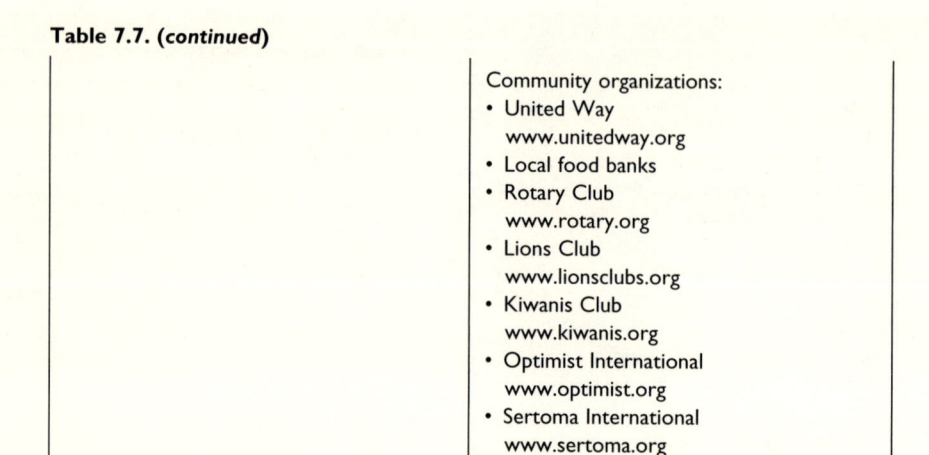

	Community organizations:
	• United Way
	  www.unitedway.org
	• Local food banks
	• Rotary Club
	  www.rotary.org
	• Lions Club
	  www.lionsclubs.org
	• Kiwanis Club
	  www.kiwanis.org
	• Optimist International
	  www.optimist.org
	• Sertoma International
	  www.sertoma.org

FINAL THOUGHTS AND REFLECTIONS

In chapters 1 and 3 we defined civility as politeness and incivility as rudeness. Public education has a long-standing history of efforts to promote civility among students. Various states have initiatives and programs that mandate teachers and others to make civility a goal for students to demonstrate. Yet, civility is often times the first attribute that breaks down when adversity arises or when groups and individual students recognize the power they have to affect others. The experiences, ideals, principles, and practices that we foster in our classrooms should promote the best of our humanity—the intentional actions that reflect respect, care, and harmony.

Certainly civility and incivility can positively and negatively affect the school and classroom cultures in a profound way. It may even affect the relationships between students, parents, teachers, administrators, and colleagues. The lessons offered in this chapter provide examples for how one might use the MOI to begin the thinking process for various grades. While we use the term lesson plan, these plans could be developed into a larger project or used to design a school-wide initiative. You may wish to consider the following questions as conversation starters, or reflect on these questions and statements as they relate to your own experiences.

Questions for Consideration:

- How have you experienced civility and incivility in your classroom and school?

- How have each affected the school and classroom culture?
- How has civility been addressed at the classroom level?
- How has civility been addressed school-wide?
- How have initiatives regarding civility affected change?
- Civility requires one to be proactive and actively engaged in promoting behaviors, speech, and actions that are appropriate and supportive. How might your school promote civility in the community and be a catalyst for change?

Write comments or notes here:

_____

_____

_____

_____

_____

_____

_____

ACTION PLAN TEMPLATE

Table 7.8.

Name of Project	
Statement of Need (why did you choose this project?)	
Outcome (what do you wish to have happen as a result of your actions?)	
Getting Started (what are your beginning steps?)	<ul><li></li><li></li><li></li><li></li></ul>
Next Steps (how will you sustain your actions?)	<ul><li></li><li></li><li></li><li></li><li></li></ul>
Impact on Others (describe your actual results related to others)	
Impact on you (how did this work affect you?)	

8

LESSON PLANS IN COMPASSION

In this chapter, our readers are asked to explore lessons on the teaching of compassion, the second characteristic. As in chapter 7, we have written four lessons, one for each grade range: K–2, 3–5, 6–8, and 9–12. Some of the lessons are designed to be taught in one or two sittings. Others may take several weeks. We have followed the same format introduced in chapter 7, with each lesson addressing the overall goal, specific objective, and focus level from the Model of Influence. Just as with the lessons on civility, the lessons on compassion can also be slightly changed, in some instances, to address another of the three characteristics, which are the focus of this book. With a little creativity and adaptation, the lessons can also serve as a framework for teaching other character traits, such as gratitude or kindness.

The lessons on compassion utilize a variety of learning styles and processes for teaching. For instance, in the K–2 lesson, students are asked to use a graphic organizer, a word web, to deepen their understanding of the word, compassion. The 3–5 lesson asks students to create a digital poster in groups of three or four. For the 6–8 lesson, students are asked to select from a number of options, a means to express themselves regarding various beliefs and feelings about compassion. In the high school lesson, students use a selection of quotations from famous individuals as a catalyst for community influence.

We invite our readers to modify or adapt these lessons in any way he or she sees fit. Some may be covered in a single lesson; others may take several days, or even weeks, to fully explore. As with all of our ideas, we hope that these suggested lessons provide a foundation on which to build an entire system with deeply embedded teaching of these critical characteristics. As with chapter 7, we offer some final thoughts and questions at the end of the chapter to reflect upon and use as possible conversation starters. We encourage the reader to think about their personal and professional experiences as they ponder each question.

COMPASSION LESSON PLAN: K–2

Goal: Help students understand what it means to be **COMPASSIONATE** and how to demonstrate compassion in and out of the classroom.

Objective: Define compassion, engage in discussion about compassion, and demonstrate acts of caring and compassion.

Focus Level: 1 and 2 (Developing Consciousness and Acknowledging and Affirming Beliefs)

Table 8.1.

Lesson Content	
Assessments: Students will create a word web that represents compassion.	
Procedures:	**Materials, Supplies, and Resources:**
Instructional set • Explain to students that the lesson will introduce a new vocabulary word, compassion. Tell them that they will be able to define it and tell what compassion looks like, feels like, and sounds like. Content • Open a discussion about what students think compassion means. Give examples of synonyms to help them make connections. Provide students with a definition. • Give examples of what compassion might look and feel like in the classroom.	• *Wilfrid Gordon McDonald Partridge* by Mem Fox. • Flipchart paper • Graphic organizer—web • Related words on cards (for additional activities in notes)

Procedures:	Materials, Supplies, and Resources:
• Read *Wilfrid Gordon McDonald Partridge* by Mem Fox. Give students a preview of the book. Ask them to pay attention to when Wilfrid might be showing compassion. Stop periodically to ask question. *Example questions: How do we know Wilfrid cared about the people next door? In what way was Ms. Nancy troubled? How did Wilfrid respond to her? What did he do to help her? Why did he want to help her? How did her show compassion? What did he do to show compassion? How do you think Wilfrid felt when he helped Ms. Nancy? How did Ms. Nancy respond?* Ask students to transfer their understanding of *compassion to the classroom? How could they be like Wilfrid and show compassion toward one another, their family, neighbors, and friends?* • Create a word web. Tell students they need to identify five words that represent or relate to compassion. Have students tell why they selected those words. Write the words on a flip chart paper or use a graphic organizer to record students' work. *Note: Another activity would be to have related words on cards and have students work with a partner or a small group to sort and organize words that relate to compassion.* Closing • Review the definition and why compassion is important in and out of the classroom. Review key parts of the book to illustrate compassion.	

Table 8.2.

Level Extensions: (ideas for applications for next three levels)	None for this lesson
Home and Community Connections: (possible organizations, ideas to do with parents, ways it is demonstrated outside of school)	• Create a compassion jar. Each time a student observes someone showing compassion the student will place a "compassion chip in the jar." At the end of the week, or daily, you can count the chips or ask students to recount why they placed the chip in the jar. This could be done at home or in the classroom.
Grade Modifications: (ideas for other grades)	
Kindergarten • Draw a picture that represents compassion. Have students write a sentence that describes the picture. If they cannot write, have students present their pictures to the class and explain the meaning. • Share a time when they were compassionate to their friend or sibling. Ask them how it made them and the other person feel.	Second Grade • Integrate math and use the word web to create a list of reoccurring words. Use those words to create a class motto related to compassion. • Identify one way they can show compassion in the classroom or at home.

COMPASSION LESSON PLAN: 3–5

Goal: Help students understand what it means to be **COMPASSIONATE** and how to demonstrate compassion in and out of the classroom.

Objective: Identify acts of compassion, kindness, and caring through historical or current events media outlets. Transfer and demonstrate their knowledge of compassion in the classroom.

Focus Level: 1 and 2 (Developing Consciousness and Acknowledging and Affirming Beliefs)

Note: This lesson is based on an assumption that students have a general understanding of compassion and can identify actions, behaviors, and acts of compassion. If not, that would be the first lesson. This lesson also might be best organized as a project.

Table 8.3.

Lesson Content	
Assessments: Students will create and present a compassion poster.	
Procedures:	**Materials, Supplies, and Resources:**
Instructional set • Explain to students that the lesson will build on their understanding of compassion. Tell them that they will be able to define and identify acts of compassion in various ways. Tell students they will work in groups to create and present a poster that demonstrates their understanding. Content • Review the meaning of compassion. Ask students to identify words or phrases that reflect compassion. Provide a few examples and explain how the words or phrases relate to compassion. For example: caring or showing consideration. • Provide examples of where students might see compassion displayed in school/classroom. A recent example that relates specifically to the class would add relevance to the discussion. Also, provide examples (video clips, newspaper articles, blogs posting, etc.) of how compassion is displayed in the environment, at home or community, and among people. • Discuss each example with students. Ask them to tell why and how that example defines compassion. • Divide students into groups of 4. Tell the students they are going to work together to create a digital poster that reflects how compassion is exhibited in the environment, with people, in the school/classroom, and at home. • Groups will present their posters to the class. Note: Allow students to self-select to decide how they want to complete the project. Give options for students to divide the assignment into quadrants and look for specific examples for each. Students might also look for several examples for each quadrant and choose the best one or ones that represent each category. Closing • Review the definition and lesson regarding compassion. Clarify any questions regarding the poster project.	• Videos clips, news stories, photos, etc., that depict compassion. • Computers with internet access. • Digital poster software. For example, glogster or Prezi might be good options. **For Teachers:** **How would you modify this lesson to meet the needs of your students?** **Alternative materials, resources?**

Table 8.4.

Level Extensions:	• Write a reflection or journal about how this project helped them (the student) understand the concept of compassion. Reflect on the following: Why is it important to show compassion toward others? • Describe how they have shown compassion to others, in the community and for the environment, or how they plan to demonstrate compassion in those areas.
Home and Community Connections:	• Send information home to parents about the poster project to help students locate examples in the home where compassion might be exampled. This would also apply to the community. • Have students locate local organizations that reflect compassion for others in need.

Grade Modifications:

Third Grade	Fifth Grade
• Have them describe a time when someone has shown them compassion or when they have shown compassion toward someone else. • Create an acronym or anagrams using compassion. • Create a class motto related to compassion. Have students define it, create examples of appropriate behaviors and actions, and consequences when compassion is not displayed.	• Divide students in small groups. Have each group research one to two organizations that reflect the idea of compassion. Ask students to find out what kinds of programs the organizations may already have underway that the class might become involved with. Present the information to class. Choose an organization for a future service-learning project.

COMPASSION LESSON PLAN: GRADES 6–8

Goal: Help students clearly define for themselves what **COMPASSION** looks like, feels like, and sounds like through self-expression using a variety of media, and assist them in deepening their commitment to living with compassion for themselves and others.

Objective: Define compassion through a variety of media.

Focus Level: Level 1 and 2 (Developing Consciousness and Acknowledging & Affirming Beliefs)

Table 8.5.

Lesson Content
Assessments: Students will express their personal definitions as well as beliefs about compassion through their choice from a variety of means of self-expression. Choices include art, music, drama, and other forms of media.

Procedures:	Materials, Supplies, and Resources:
Instructional set • Tell students they will explore the meaning of compassion, exclusion, and inclusion through sharing personal experiences as well as choosing ways to express their definitions and beliefs using a variety of media.	• Art supplies (paper, markers, paints, brushes, colored pencils, etc.) • Student journals
Content • Begin the lesson by asking students to quietly reflect on a time when they were excluded. Consider sharing possible instances of exclusion many have experienced. • When students have identified an instance or two, ask them to write down the details of the exclusion: how they felt, what they thought, and any other thoughts or memories they have about the event(s). • In pairs or small groups, ask students to share, as they are willing, their experiences. Working with them, help them identify commonalities from their experiences. Ask them to focus on the feelings their experiences evoked, both then and now. • Have students share their collective thoughts, as they are willing, and as they share, write their responses on a whiteboard or other surface. • Define compassion (concern for others), exclusion (being left off or left out), and inclusion (being a part of, being accepted). • Ask students to identify how compassion relates to the act of excluding and including. Help them see the relationship if needed (when we act with compassion, we increase the likelihood that others will be included; we also likely become more caring individuals).	*Note: Consider these examples: being left off a birthday invitation list, not being asked to sit with a group at lunch, finding out about an activity where others participated after it happened, being left out of a group text. Emphasize that everyone has been excluded at some time. Other examples may be evident and more relevant.* *Note: You may need to share personal examples or other examples from the school community that bring more relevance to this discussion.*

Table 8.5. *(continued)*

Procedures:	Materials, Supplies, and Resources:

• While referring to the experiences they shared, ask students to think about how they felt different from others when they were left out. Ask students to think about those who are different as a result of disability, ethnicity, religion, race, culture, or other factor.
• Have students share their thoughts about being significantly different from those around you, again emphasizing that all feel excluded and different at times.
• Ask students how the concept of compassion relates to the differences they have discussed. Specifically, ask students to put themselves in another's shoes and ask them to express how they wish to be treated when they are different from those around them. This may be done in a small group or as a class.
• Inform students that they will explore compassion through a variety of media as they move into the next part of the lesson sequence.
• Make the point that just as we are all different, we all express ourselves best in different ways.
• Through their choices of projects, ask students to personally define compassion, using descriptive words that express how compassion feels, looks, and sounds, and to incorporate their personal definitions within their projects.
• From the list provided below, ask students to choose a means of expression concerning their beliefs and feelings related to compassion. Add other choices as appropriate.
   1. Draw what compassion feels like.
   2. Write a story that illustrates compassion.
   3. Take a series of photographs that represent compassion.
   4. Work with others to write a short play that demonstrates compassion.
	This may also be a time during which the school counselor may have some suggestions for addressing these issues.
	
	For Teachers:
	How would you modify this lesson to meet the needs of your students? Alternative materials, resources?
	
	Note: These choices appeal to a variety of learning styles. Other options may be added as needed to meet student interests or ways of expressing themselves.

LESSON PLANS IN COMPASSION

Procedures:	Materials, Supplies, and Resources:
5. Interview someone who has lived a compassionate life. 6. Create a collage that represents compassion. • Ask students to share their various projects and how their beliefs about exclusion, inclusion, and compassion have changed or evolved through the lesson(s). Closing • Review the concepts of inclusion, exclusion, and their relationship to compassion. Ask students to briefly share how their understanding of compassion has changed. Invite them to observe themselves and others for additional examples of compassionate behaviors, noting how it feels, looks, and sounds.	

Table 8.6.

Level Extensions: (ideas for applications for next three levels) Level 3 (Realizing Benefits to Self and Others)	• Ask students to keep a journal of their experiences and observations regarding inclusion, exclusion, and compassionate responses. Have them to make note of the consequences of acts of compassion on the recipients as well as the individual who exhibits compassion. Have students particularly notice when they are the ones on the receiving end. Ask them to reflect on how acts of compassion shape their perspectives and beliefs. • Periodically, have students share their observations in class with small groups and/or with the entire class.

Table 8.6. (*continued*)

Level 4 (Taking Action and Embracing Influence)	• As students journal, ask them to look for opportunities to act in compassionate ways, consistent with their beliefs. Have them notice the consequences of their compassionate acts toward others. Encourage students to note how being compassionate toward others affects their thoughts and feelings. • Have students note how their acts of compassionate behavior influence those around them. As students keep their journals, ask them to share their observations regularly.
Home and Community Connections: (possible organizations, ideas to do with parents, ways it is demonstrated outside of school)	• Have students identify another or a group of others who are different from themselves in some way. • Suggest that students seek specific ways to include those who are different in activities outside the school environment. Perhaps they might work with a Sunday school class to help with students who have disabilities, or they might volunteer to read to an elderly housebound adult. They might volunteer to have conversations with children of families who are homeless or from migrant families. The emphasis should be on demonstrating care and concern for others, through acts that embrace and include.

COMPASSION LESSON PLAN: GRADES 9–12

Goal: Help students to develop a deep understanding of **COMPASSION** by using beliefs, actions, and lives of famous figures to serve as a catalyst for applying that understanding to their various communities.

Objective: Identify and apply characteristics of compassion in local communities.

Focus Level: 3 and 4 (Realizing Benefits to Self and Others and Taking Action and Embracing Influence)

Table 8.7.

Lesson Content
Assessments: Students will reflect on characteristics of compassion through discussion and/or journaling, conduct and report on research about famous individuals demonstrating compassion, and participate in self-selected opportunity to demonstrate compassion through their community.

Procedures:	Materials, Supplies, and Resources:
Instructional set • Tell students that they will be examining the words and lives of famous individuals concerning compassion. Additionally, students will be asked to demonstrate "Ubuntu" (described later, meaning sharing our universal bond) in their community(ies). Content • Select a quote, either from the list presented on the right or from other sources, and ask students to listen to the quote as you read it. • Ask students to reflect on these questions: What feelings did the quote evoke? What thoughts did the quote evoke? What does compassion look like in the world? What are the consequences of compassionate acts? What are the consequences of a lack of compassion? Student reflections may be made orally or in a journal. • Have students conduct research on the individual who made the quote, seeking to identify the qualities of the individual that might have contributed to the quote. This may be done in pairs, as a small group, or as individuals. Some suggested topics/questions to explore include: Briefly describe the famous figure's life. How did the famous figure demonstrate compassion? What barriers did he/she encounter? What is he/she most well-known for? How did his/her compassionate influence shape the world? What other qualities/ characteristics would you use to describe him/her? What beliefs and perspectives do you believe he/she	Selected Quotes by Famous Individuals: • *Love and compassion are necessities, not luxuries. Without them humanity cannot survive.* Dalai Lama • *Our task must be to free ourselves by widening our circle of compassion to embrace all living creatures and the whole of nature and its beauty.* Albert Einstein • *Mama was my greatest teacher, a teacher of compassion, love and fearlessness. If love is sweet as a flower, then my mother is that sweet flower of love.* Stevie Wonder • *My mission in life is not merely to survive, but to thrive; and to do so with some passion, some compassion, some humor, and some style.* Maya Angelou • *Our human compassion binds us the one to the other—not in pity or patronizingly—but as human beings who have learnt how to turn our common suffering into hope for the future.* Nelson Mandela • *The purpose of human life is to serve, and to show compassion and the will to help others.* Albert Schweitzer Websites: • Academy of Achievement www.achievement.org • Nelson Mandela on "Ubuntu" www.youtube.com/watch?v=HED4h00xPPA • Archbishop Desmond Tutu on "Ubuntu" http://www*

Table 8.7. (*continued*)

held? How might you apply this famous figure's principles and beliefs to your own life? • Consider asking students, individually or in groups, to share what they have learned about various individuals. • Through a discussion, compare and contrast famous individuals. You may wish to use a visual means such as a T-Chart or other graphic organizer to do this Ask: How were they similar? How were they different? In what ways did each represent compassion? • After students have examined famous individuals and their legacy regarding compassion, introduce them to the concept of "Ubuntu," an African (Nguni Bantu or Southern African language) philosophy that means that we share a universal bond connecting all humanity. Although the concept was practiced by Nelson Mandela, Archbishop Desmond Tutu has described a person with Ubuntu as someone who welcomes others, shows a willingness to be vulnerable, affirms others, does not feel threatened by others, and recognizes that we are a part of a greater whole. • Ask students for examples when the characteristics identified by Tutu have been observed in the school, the community, state, and world. • Discuss, if appropriate, the relationship between civility and compassion. Being respectful (civility) is certainly the beginning to welcoming others (compassion). • Ask students to identify situations where they might demonstrate Ubuntu. • Compile a list representing a variety of ideas. Have students individually write about how they might demonstrate the characteristics as described by Tutu through a chosen situation. • Inform students that they have an opportunity to influence the community in which they live by demonstrating Ubuntu. • Ask them to begin planning how they wish to get started. Closing • Periodically revisit their work, inviting them to share with the class and others the benefits to selves and others of their actions.	*Note: Students may conduct brief research using the Academy of Achievement website which profiles extraordinary leaders who have shaped the world.* *Note: There may be other more appropriate means of visual representation of information shared. The T-Chart is only one of many ways to generate discussion.* *Note: For a video clip on Nelson Mandela see resources listed at the beginning of this lesson. Also see quote from Tutu in the same list.* **For Teachers:** **How would you modify this lesson to meet the needs of your students? Alternative materials, resources?**

Table 8.8.

Level Extensions: (ideas for applications for next three levels)	Note: This lesson series is designed to begin at Level 3 (Realizing Benefits to Self and Others) and to extend into Level 4 (Taking Action and Embracing Influence). It is assumed that most students in grades 9–12 will be ready to participate fully in the ideas presented. If students do not seem to be ready, the reader is referred to the lesson plan designed for middle school (grades 6–8) presented earlier in this chapter.
Home and Community Connections: (possible organizations, ideas to do with parents, ways it is demonstrated outside of school)	• Ask students to identify a situation or situations where they might have influence in embracing Ubuntu. They might begin by welcoming others new to school, especially those who are different. They might volunteer at a local shelter or food bank. Numerous opportunities exist through family, neighborhood, and community to demonstrate the qualities of Ubuntu.

FINAL THOUGHTS AND REFLECTIONS

In earlier chapters we defined compassion and being kind, considerate, caring for others, and empathizing. As our students navigate an ever increasing non-compassionate world, we need to empower them to be change agents—difference makers who respond to the wrongs in society, the school, and even the classroom in a strong and resolute manner. Certainly, teachers, parents, and other concerned persons can model those behaviors, but students need opportunities—real authentic opportunities to experience what compassion looks and feels like. It is through those experiences that their thinking is challenged or affirmed. It is through those experiences that they explore their own actions toward creating better outcomes for others. Compassion is a universal necessity to activate care, humanitarianism, risk taking, and hope. The lessons offered in this chapter are suggestions for how one might begin implementing such change in their classrooms and schools.

As with the previous chapter, we end the chapter with some questions to consider and reflect upon. These questions can be used as conversation starters or simply questions to help you reflect upon your feelings about teaching compassion or integrating compassion into the school's and classroom's curriculum. The overall goal is to examine your beliefs and embrace your influence as difference maker in the classroom and in the school.

Questions for Consideration:

- When have you shown great compassion toward a student?
- How did that (showing compassion) change the student's behavior, actions, or thinking?
- What effect did the demonstration of compassionate behavior have on you?
- Think of a time when you witnessed a resistance to show a student compassion. It may have been a situation involving a parent, another student, or colleague. How did you respond?
- Would you have done anything differently? If so, what would you have done? If not, how did you respond to that student's needs?
- There are many local, and perhaps global, organizations that are missioned to be compassionate to those in need. Can you think of any organization in your local community that might be an effective partner?
- How might you integrate this organization into your classroom or school curriculum?

Write comments or notes here:

_____
_____
_____
_____
_____
_____

9

LESSON PLANS IN COURAGE

This is the final chapter focusing on lesson plans. In many respects, these lessons on courage were the most difficult to write. We asked ourselves, how do you help students examine that which may frighten them? Many adults have difficulty with that. As we defined it in chapters 1 and 3, courage begins with a tentative yet bold step in the face of adversity. How do we explain that to a first or second grade child? How do we ask our students to not only develop a consciousness and affirm beliefs as they explore the meaning of courage, but also to realize benefit to self and others, and most importantly, take action and embrace influence? Whether or not we hit the mark, we believe that we did crack open the door for exploration.

The lessons provided here also follow our established format. They attempt to give students a variety of experiences, using several different teaching processes as well as learning styles. The K–2 lesson asks students to begin defining what courage means. In the 3–5 lesson, students create a digital comic about courage. Students in grades 6–8 explore courage through film and books. A suggested list of both is included in the lesson. In grades 9–12, students are asked to engage in deep reflection of fear and journal about how courage helps one overcome fear.

It goes without saying that the lessons are designed to be used specifically for the characteristic of courage, but as we worked on them, in many cases it was evident that courage sometimes encompasses compassion, and sometimes civility. At any rate, we found elements of the characteristic compassion in almost every lesson on courage. In our lessons, at times we even suggest that our readers ask students to look at the content through the lens of both characteristics. After all, what is most important, that students can define the characteristics and provide pure examples, or that students begin with the development of consciousness and end with the embracing of their influence on the world? We encourage the reader to reflect upon the conversation starters and questions at the end of the chapter. Think about how your experiences have helped you demonstrate courage and how you might help students embrace that attribute and use it in their own lives to respond to adversity.

COURAGE LESSON PLAN: K–2

Goal: Help students understand what it means to be **COURAGE** and how to take positive steps even when frightened or faced with adversity.

Objective: Identify acts of courage in and out of the classroom. Students will also define courage and provide examples of courage in the classroom.

Focus Level: 1 and 2 (Developing Consciousness and Acknowledging and Affirming Beliefs)

Note: A first lesson might be defining and identifying courage and courageous actions and people. This lesson is also one that might be best organized as a project.

Table 9.1.

Lesson Content	
Assessments: Students will identify actions and behaviors that are examples of courage in the world and in the classroom.	
Procedures:	**Materials, Supplies, and Resources:**
Instructional set • Explain to students that the lesson will introduce them to courageous people in their communities, and what courageous actions and behaviors look like. Content • Define courage and provide students with other words related to courage.	• Video clips or photographs representing courage. • Discussion questions • Presentation with examples of courageous acts and contrasting acts.

Procedures:

- Explain what courage traditionally looks like outside of the classroom.
Note: Show a video clip of someone being courageous.
- Explain what courage means in the classroom. Provide examples of actions and behaviors that might illustrate courage. *For example: the courage to ask questions; the courage to speak up for someone else who is afraid; the courage to question when something does feel right or look right; the courage to do the right thing even when you might be alone.*

- Engage in a discussion of the following examples of courageous and foolish acts. Ask students to categorize each pairing.

Examples:
1. Fighting or walking away from a fight
2. Doing something dangerous that others are doing or not participating even if someone calls you "chicken"
3. Teasing and bullying someone or standing up for someone who is being mistreated
4. Blaming others for your mistakes or accepting responsibility
5. Ignoring a new student or making friends with a new student
6. Only looking out for yourself or helping others
7. Following the crowd or doing what's right
8. Quitting when things get tough or working hard, even when it's difficult

- Ask students to journal about a time when they were courageous or when they witnessed someone's courageous actions and/or behavior.

<u>Closing</u>
- Review the definition and examples of courage. Add words to word list or word web.

Materials, Supplies, and Resources:

For Teachers:
How would you modify this lesson to meet the needs of your students? Alternative materials, resources?
Note: Consider making the courageous and contrasting acts more hands-on. Pass out cards with the examples on them. Have students find their partner and explain why and/or how the two relate. Also might consider having students explain why the more positive one would benefit self and others (Level 3).

Table 9.2.

Level Extensions	See teacher notes for level 3 idea.
Home and Community Connections: (possible organizations, ideas to do with parents, ways it is demonstrated outside of school)	• See grade modification ideas. • Organize families to have a lemonade stand to raise funds for a deserving organization. See the article "Change for Change: A Lemonade Stand for Action" by Mark Cooper and Candice Dowd Barnes
Grade Modifications	

Kindergarten	First Grade
• Integrate art. Partner with an organization such as: https://www.facebook.com/ButterfliesForCourageous Kids. Have students make butterflies and or butterfly collages to send to other children. Consider combining with the concept of compassion.	• Introduce organizations that promote courage among children. Such as: Kids of Courage—https://www.kidsoc.org/ Make a Wish—http://wish.org • Have students read two different books or stories about courage. Contrast the stories and present a book review or report.

COURAGE LESSON PLAN: 3–5

Goal: Help students understand what it means to be **COURAGE** and how to take positive steps even when frightened or faced with adversity.

Objective: Students will define and explain what courage looks and feels like. Students will create a visual and digital depiction that reflects courage.

Focus Level: 1 and 2 (Developing Consciousness and Acknowledging and Affirming Beliefs)

Note: A first lesson might be defining and identifying courage and courageous actions and people. This lesson is also one that might be best organized as a project.

Table 9.3.

Lesson Content	
Assessments: Students will create a comic that tells a story of a heroic figure and how the character displays courage.	
Procedures:	**Materials, Supplies, and Resources:**
Instructional set • Explain to students that the lesson will build on their understanding of courage and how one shows courage. Tell students they will create a comic about courage. *Note: There are several types of comic creator software. See the resources list for one that might work for your students. Suggested comic creator is Pixton.* Content (step-by-step procedures) • Facilitate a mini-lesson on the meaning of courage. Ask students to recall or generate examples of courage. • Discuss the importance of being courageous. • Discuss how courage is displayed in the classroom. For example, share scenarios that illustrate a student who shows courage to ask questions on an assignment even though that student might have been uncomfortable or frightened. Provide another scenario that might have been a part of a recent news headline or a historical event that illustrates courageous actions or behaviors. • Ask student to generate a list of words that relate to courage and why those words were selected. • Assuming that one of the words is hero, engage in a more substantive conversation about the characteristics of a hero. Explain what a hero is and does and provide some examples of real and fictional heroes. *Note: Consider having students research historical figures who exemplified courage and ask them to report on why those people were courageous and what characteristics made them courageous.* Introduce the comic assignment. Students can work individually or in pairs to create a comic about a hero who demonstrates courage. Closing Review the definition and lesson regarding courage. Clarify any questions regarding the assignment.	• Comic creator software. Comic creator software resources: http://www.pixton.com http://MakeBeliefsComix.com http://www.toondoo.com **For Teachers:** **How would you modify this lesson to meet the needs of your students? Alternative materials, resources?** *Note: A first step might be for each student or dyad to develop the characters first and a backstory. A second step might be for students to familiarize themselves with the comic creator software they will use to create the comic. Collaborate with the I/T person in your school.*

Table 9.4.

Level Extensions:	See the third grade modification. This activity could be used to engage students at level 3 or 4.
Home and Community Connections:	• Conduct an internet search for hometown heroes. Have students describe why that person is heroic, what acts of courage they demonstrated, and what is inspiring about their story.
Grade Modifications	

Third Grade	Fourth Grade
• Students work with a partner or in a small group to identify five ways they can show courage in the classroom.	• See Home/Community connections section. Students can present their work to the class.

COURAGE LESSON PLAN: GRADES 6–8

Goal: Help students develop an awareness of the characteristics of **COURAGEOUS** acts through film and/or books and shape their own beliefs about being **COURAGEOUS**.

Objective: Reflect on and shape personal beliefs about courage.

Focus Level: Level 1 and 2 (Developing a Consciousness and Acknowledging and Affirming Beliefs)

Table 9.5.

Lesson Content
Assessments: Class will develop a definition for courage, including how it looks, sounds, feels. Students will individually reflect on their own definition and beliefs about courage. In addition, they will record and report on acts of courage they have experienced.

Procedures:	Materials, Supplies, and Resources:
Instructional set • Tell students that they are going to identify characteristics of courage through book and film, while shaping their own beliefs. Content • Ask students what it means to them to have courage. What does courage look like? Sound like? Feel like? Record their collective thoughts.	Movies : • *Pay It Forward* (PG-13, 2000) A young boy tries to make the world a better place after his teacher gives him the chance. • *Mighty Joe Young* (PG, 1998) This Disney movie is about courageously advocating for an animal, the gorilla Joe. • *Rudy* (PG, 1993) A high school student ends up becoming a walk-on despite his small stature and initially dismal prospects.

Procedures:

- Ask for examples of courageous behaviors they have witnessed or exhibited. How did these look? Sound? Feel?
- Develop a definition for courage with the class. Simply put, courage is the strength to do something that frightens you.
- Collectively, decide how you recognize courage.
- Select from film, literature, or other forms of media, stories of courage. A suggested list is provided on the right under materials, supplies, and resources.
- Books can be read aloud to class, little by little, assigned as homework, or even incorporated into a literature, science, or social studies unit.
- Film can be used similarly. It is not necessary that the film or book be viewed in one or two sittings. What is most important is that looking for courageous acts be a primary focus.
- As each portion of the book is read or film is viewed, engage students in discussion about acts of courage noted, returning to the definition posed by the class. Ask what does this look like, sound like, feel like?
- As class works through book/film, reexamine the definition written by the class. Ask if there are elements that should be added/deleted/changed.
- At the conclusion of the book/film, inform students that they will be keeping a journal on acts of courage.
- Have students observe others as well as themselves, looking for and recording events and acts of courage. Ask them to include what they have witnessed as well as how it makes them feel and think.
- As students reflect on what they have noted, introduce the notion of affirming their own beliefs about courage.

Closing
- Have students reflect on how their beliefs have changed through the course of this exploration. Have students select and report on what they have witnessed as well as the impact this has had on their beliefs and perspectives.

Materials, Supplies, and Resources:

- *Rudy* (PG, 1993) A high school student ends up becoming a walk-on despite his small stature and initially dismal prospects.
- *Radio* (PG) The true story of Robert "Radio" Kennedy, a story of dreaming and standing up for what one believes.
- *October Sky* (PG, 1999) Despite multiple setbacks, a high school student is inspired to make rockets.

Books:
- *Fire from the Rock* by Sharon Draper (interest level 4th–7th) Sylvia Patterson is chosen to be one of the first black students to attend Central High School in Little Rock, AR.
- *Number the Stars* by Lois Lowry (interest level 5th–8th) Annemarie risks her own life to save another's during the Holocaust.
- *The Wanderer* by Sharon Creech (interest level 3rd–6th) A thirteen-year-old is the only girl on a dangerous but adventurous sailing voyage across the Atlantic.
- *The True Confessions of Charlotte Doyle* by Avi (interest level 5th–8th) An action-filled tale of courage and adventure on the high seas.
- *Hatchet* by Gary Paulsen (interest level 6th and up) When his plane crashes in the Canadian wilderness, Brian learns patience and courage to face his situation.
- Other books can be found at https://www.the-best-childrens-books.org
- Student journals

For Teachers:
How would you modify this lesson to meet the needs of your students? Alternative materials, resources?

Table 9.6.

Level Extensions: (ideas for applications for next three levels) Level 3 (Realizing Benefits to Self and Others)	• As students reflect on and shape their beliefs about courage, ask them to include reflections in their journals about the benefits for both the one who acts courageously and the recipient(s) or beneficiaries of the courageous act. • Ask students to incorporate new understandings into their beliefs. • As a class, review students' new understandings, and revise class definition as appropriate.
Level 4 (Taking Action and Embracing Influence)	• As in Level 3, ask students to incorporate into their journals how they might take action. • As a class discussion, ask students to revisit those acts of courage witnessed or experienced. Revisit the characteristics that made them acts of courage. • Engage them in dialogue about how they might begin to take small steps, and identify instances where courage might be called for: speaking up to ask a question, spending time with a student who is not typically embraced by peers, asking for help, doing something new and perhaps a bit frightening for the first time, etc. • Ask each student to identify an instance where he or she might take action. • Have students process action steps with a partner or small group. • Ask students to select a targeted timeframe and setting if appropriate. • As students behave in courageous ways, celebrate successes and victories.
Home and Community Connections: (possible organizations, ideas to do with parents, ways it is demonstrated outside of school)	• Have students find a trusted adult or family member to share their journals with. Have students engage in dialogue with their family member or trusted adult about acts of courage seen by them.

COURAGE LESSON PLAN: GRADES 9–12

Goal: Assist students to examine the concepts of fear and **COURAGE** within a personal context through the use of quotes by others as well as events or stories that have served to highlight **COURAGEOUS** acts in the face of fear.

Objective: Use personal fears as a way to personalize the meaning of courage.

Focus Levels: 2 and 3 (Acknowledging and Affirming Beliefs and Realizing Benefits to Self and Others)

Table 9.7.

Lesson Content
Assessments: Students will reflect, in writing, their insights on the meaning of courage as it applies to their individual lives. Additionally, as an extension, students will write a speech, letter, or develop another means of presentation to address a local issue or concern within their school or community.

Procedures:	Materials, Supplies, and Resources:
Instructional set • Tell students that they will be individually defining courage within the context of the exploration of their own fears. As an extension, students will be asked to participate in a project that takes courage into action. Content • This lesson begins with the examination of the concept of fear. • Using the quote to the right by Ralph Waldo Emerson, ask students to quietly reflect on the message in the quote. This may be completed in a journal or orally, depending on the dynamics of the class. • Invite students to identify that which they fear and to write about it through a journal entry. • Ask students to describe in their journals **how** they feel when they are afraid. For example, some may be afraid of spiders, snakes, public speaking, flying, or even asking someone out on a date. • Ask students to describe the physical symptoms. Some physical symptoms may include headaches, stomachaches, pounding heart, sweaty palms. • Ask students to share as they are willing.	Suggested Quotes: "Always, always, always do the thing you fear, and the death of fear is certain" Ralph Waldo Emerson "Courage is the resistance of fear, mastery of fear—not the absence of fear" Mark Twain "Courage: the most important of all the virtues because without courage, you can't practice any other virtues consistently." Maya Angelou "Keep in mind that many people have died for their beliefs; it's actually quite common. The real courage is in living and suffering for what you believe." Christopher Paolini Student journals

Table 9.7. *(continued)*

Procedures:	Materials, Supplies, and Resources:
• Explore the concept of courage. Ask students to define courage. Is courage standing up for what they believe? Is it daring to be different? Is it remaining quiet or not acting? • Engage in a class discussion about the meaning of fear and its relationship to courage. How are they alike? How are they different? Must one always have fear in order to have courage? • Use recent media events to more deeply explore elements of fear and courage. • Ask students to share examples of the demonstration of courage from the media or their community. • With each example cited, discuss how those involved responded to fear and how courage was demonstrated. • Return the discussion to Emerson's quote, asking if students believe that the "death of fear" occurred in each example. Ask if it is important to eradicate fear. Why or why not? • At the end of this part of the discussion, ask students to return to their journals and to reread their entries about fear, then ask them to reflect and add new insights from the discussion of courage and the meaning of Emerson's quote. • Ask students to share their new insights as they are willing. • At this point, you may wish to explore the quote by Maya Angelou, which suggests that courage is foundational to the development of all other "virtues." What does this mean? Do students believe this is true? Why or why not? Are there character traits (virtues) that can be developed without courage as the foundation? Discuss these questions with the class. • With students, discuss the relationship of civility and compassion to courage. Closing • At the conclusion of the discussion, ask students if they are willing to more deeply explore their own fears and the ways in which they might demonstrate courage. Invite students to again reflect on their initial entries and to reflect on initial steps they might take to address their fears. • Suggest that students note progress and struggles as they work through their individual fears.	*Note: It may be appropriate to discuss the science related to the physical symptoms of fear. A school counselor may also be invited to assist with a discussion of fear and its related symptoms.* *Note: Some examples from the media may include the events surrounding 9-11, rescue efforts, civil rights or disability rights struggles, issues involving overcoming abuse. There may also be more relevant events from the school or local community.* *Note: This and other quotes are identified under the materials and resources section.* **For Teachers:** **How would you modify this lesson to meet the needs of your students? Alternative materials, resources?**

Table 9.8.

Level Extensions: (ideas for applications for next three levels)	*Note: You may wish to have students work in small groups or as a whole class, depending on the issues/concerns that are addressed.*
Level 4 (Taking Action and Embracing Influence)	• As students process and address their self-identified fears, working to take courageous steps, ask them to identify, as a group, a school or community concern or issue that may necessitate bold steps to remedy. Such issues may include inserting a stop sign at a dangerous intersection, installing a handicap-accessible playground at a nearby park or school, speaking up at a school board meeting about a safety issue, asking for a more inclusive high school function. • Have students develop a persuasive speech, letter, or other means of presentation that addresses the concern including reasons why the concern has been identified by them. Include in the speech or letter a proposed plan to remedy the concern or issue. • As students deliver their speeches, letters, etc., work with them to design next steps that may include responding with civility or compassion to resistance.
Home and Community Connections: (possible organizations, ideas to do with parents, ways it is demonstrated outside of school)	• Organizations will vary depending on issues or concerns identified with students. • Parents may be involved in a number of ways: through listening and processing in conversation, their children's fears and plans for addressing these, and/or through partnering with their children in their selected school or community project.

FINAL THOUGHTS AND REFLECTION

Courage often emotes images of superheroes—people who have suffered a particularly diminishing hardship and prevailed to save the world. In previous chapters we offered courage as demonstrating bravery in the classroom or advocating for someone else. We defined courage as acts or behaviors that can also be categorized as perseverance, determination, resistance to helplessness, and confidence.

While we acknowledge that courage might be somewhat difficult to teach, we suggest, through the example lessons, that one consider starting with an exploration of students' own beliefs, ideas, and thoughts about fear and adversity, especially in the upper grades. There is no magical solution that can activate students' learning. The magic truly lies in the responsiveness to the environment. As we discussed in earlier chapters, teachers and others must engage several strategies to ensure high levels of academic and social and emotional growth. These strategies can only be effective if one embraces and acts upon the influences they have in the lives of the students they encounter on a daily basis. Students need to be empowered to find their inner strength—their intrinsic motivation to stand up for what is right and good.

As with chapters 7 and 8, we offer some final questions and statements in this chapter to encourage you to think deeply about how you might model courage in the classroom and school. The questions might also aid in your reflecting on how courage might be activated through your instructional practices. Here are some suggested questions to use as conversation starters or to reflect upon. Think about how your personal and professional experiences exemplify courage.

Questions for Consideration

- Assume that you are working with students, many of whom lack confidence. That lack of confidence is greatly manifested through lackluster academic performance and even more so through their inability to form supportive and healthy relationships with each other. How might developing a consciousness for courage affect the students' academic performance and relationships?
- How might you model courage in the classroom or school for students to activate their confidence?
- Think about your own school experiences. Describe a time when you faced adversity and were able to overcome that challenge?

- How did you achieve success in overcoming adversity, and who played key roles in that success?
- What might you say to those persons now? How might those experiences be helpful for students facing similar challenges and struggles?
- Think about who teaches, how, and in what format are courage—bravery, confidence, and perseverance—taught or engaged in the school. On a scale of 1–10, with 10 being the best, how would you rate the implementation, sustainability, and transfer of that teaching and integration of those concepts into the school?
- If teaching courage is a challenge for you to ponder, what needs to change?

Write comments or notes here:

10

ADVICE FOR SCHOOL LEADERS

LEADER SUPPORT

While much of this book is dedicated to encouraging teachers to implement the 3C's in the classroom, school administrators, counselors, and other school leaders are also instrumental in the implementation process. Therefore, in this final chapter we offer considerations for others to ponder in support of effective implementation of these, and perhaps other, attributes into the school's curriculum. We offer these suggestions in hopes of encouraging administrators to take the necessary steps to use the Model of Influence with their staff to affect change in their school's curriculum and in the lives of the students they teach daily.

We encourage leaders to find ways to develop a consciousness regarding these attributes to enhance and support the daily curriculum. We encourage leaders to help their staff affirm their beliefs, or perhaps challenge their staff's thoughts and ideas about integrating this critical content area with their academic instruction to ensure the whole student is addressed. We offer these suggestions with the hope that leaders will guide their staff beyond the idea that implementing civility, compassion, and courage will benefit them in the classroom to acknowledging how teaching these attributes will benefit students and others as well. We offer these suggestions with the hope that leaders, teachers, counselors, and other concerned professionals will embrace the influence they have in the lives of their students. Finally, we hope they will take action to implement such a plan that will enable their students to activate these and other attributes in their lives, their families, and their communities.

In our experience, it is imperative that for any initiative to be successful the individuals at the district level must also be champions and supporters. Pockets of implementation can certainly be found without widespread support, but having an engaged, attentive, and committed central office administration and board of directors helps ensure widespread success. First, district leaders might examine policy regarding the curriculum and how social-emotional learning is embedded. Most districts have carefully crafted policies about what is taught and how students are assessed, but does your district have a policy on how social-emotional learning is supported and promoted? Second, we suggest that district leaders look at their practices regarding the formation and involvement of community partnerships. Are there community partnerships that help students learn how to become more civil, compassionate, and courageous citizens? If not, how might such partnerships be formed and supported? Lastly, we ask that all district leaders look inwardly at themselves and at the ways in which they conduct their school business. To what degree do leaders model for others the very attributes we are promoting? How are meetings conducted? Are they civil? Do they provide examples of compassion or even courage? Sometimes, the most important statement we can make is to reflect on our own behavior.

As instructional leaders in the school, oftentimes administrators and counselors have the greatest influence. They can empower and encourage their staff to integrate compassion, civility, and courage into their daily practices. They can provide resources, in-servicing, moral accountability systems, and innovative programming, all aimed at creating a school environment that uses social and emotional competencies along with the academic content to help students, teachers, and the overall school be successful.

USING THE MODEL

Remembering that the Model of Influence (MOI) is a theoretical framework that moves one from a state of developing consciousness to taking action and embracing the influence they have, we offer some key strategies and considerations for administrators and other key school leaders. With each level, one should design curriculum—lessons to build upon the previ-

ADVICE FOR SCHOOL LEADERS

- Taking Action & Embracing Influence
- Realizing Benefits to Self and Others
- Acknowledging Perspectives & Affirming Beliefs
- Developing Consciousness
- Model of Influence (MOI)

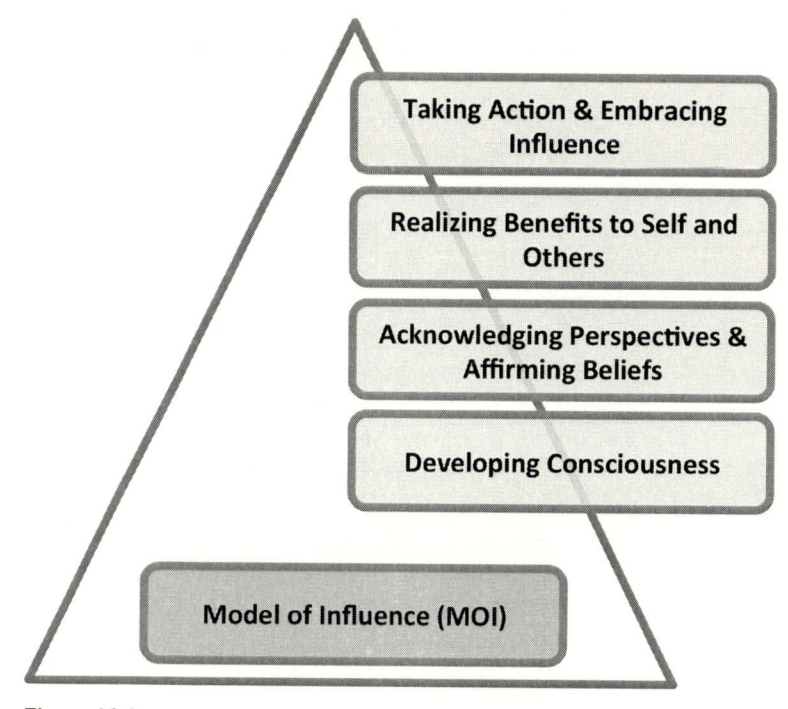

Figure 10.1.

ous level. The Model of Influence can be used to facilitate the implementation of any value, attribute, or disposition. Therefore, these key strategies can also be used and considered to facilitate discussion, reflections, and productivity toward greater, richer discourse and action.

The Model of Influence, shown above is not an add-on to instruction. While we focused on civility, compassion, and courage—three attributes sorely missing from today's classrooms—various other attributes might be exchanged and used to develop students' knowledge and move them toward action and embracing how those attributes might positively affect their lives and the lives of others. While this is not an exhaustive list of ideas for school administrators and others to consider, it offers some strategies that will support the integration of values and attributes into the school's curriculum. As you review each suggested idea, note that each is aligned to the Model of Influence in an effort to demonstrate how the model can be used. You will also see possible strategies to facilitate the promotion of other attributes necessary for developing the whole student.

Level 1—Developing Consciousness

This level is designed to facilitate knowledge building. As one develops consciousness he/she is seeking to define, reflect, and discuss how that attribute is important and essential to his/her life and the lives of others. At Level 1, the learner makes the concept and content meaningful and relevant. It is also at this level that one's thinking is challenged, enhanced, or changed depending on the level in which they begin to internalize the information into their lives. Here are a few ideas to consider related to *developing consciousness*.

- *Conversation Starters*—can be used to open a discussion with teachers and other leaders and staff about how the 3C's are reflected in the school, and perhaps, greater community. The idea is to spark some conversation that puts the concepts in the forefront of their thinking—*developing consciousness*. It moves from simple awareness that a problem exists, to thinking about how to engage in further discovery and discourse. For example, reading this book can facilitate conversations and spark an interest and motivate one to learn more, ask questions, and seek to clarify meaning.
- *Conducting research and inquiry*—is another way to deepen the thinking and enrich the conversations about this concept—further making it a part of the current consciousness or scheme of thinking. As level 1 suggests, the idea is to build interest and ask questions that lead to further discoveries, thus allowing one to move to the next level—*acknowledging perspectives and affirming beliefs*. As the administrator, presenting more information, supporting that information with research and evidence is important. Then asking the faculty and staff to invest in an inquiry process to enrich their own understanding or generate questions to facilitate further inquiry is vital to the overall process.

Level 2—Acknowledging Perspectives and Affirming Beliefs

This level addresses the idea that others' perspectives are important and carry meaning. This level serves to challenge thinking, or it might be to affirm one's current thinking or provide one with additional information to integrate in their scheme of thinking. As you are engaging in this level of the MOI, it is critical to engage in deep discussion, activities, and experiences that build upon the knowledge gained through developing consciousness. Some strategies that might be used to *affirm beliefs and acknowledge perspectives* are as follows.

- *Professional development, training, and in-servicing*—creates buy-in from faculty. Finding experts who are not only knowledgeable, but are also capable of offering teachers ways to seamlessly integrate this model into their daily teaching practices is critical. Professional development and training has the potential to challenge the current thinking and allows one to consider others' perspectives, and again, create opportunities to integrate this new information into the current thinking.
- It might also replace the current scheme and cause moments of cognitive dissonance. It is commonly understood that as one becomes frustrated by moments of misunderstanding, they are also learning. However, all professional development is not equal, and success can be enhanced through high quality, engaging, and interactive professional development that leaves teachers feeling invigorated and motivated to implement change. The ultimate goal is to move to the next level—*benefit to self and others*.
- *Assessing teachers' perspectives*—allows for the leadership to invest the appropriate amount of time, energy, effort and funding required to integrate the 3C's or other attributes into the school's curriculum. Create a survey following the professional development training to gauge your staff's opinions and perspectives of the importance, need and motivation to implement such integrated learning. Conducting a survey should provide you with valuable data to move forward. For example, you might find that your staff is comfortable with a phasing-in process. It might also reveal that the staff has some great ideas that can be implemented school-wide. The goal is to gather information that will help sustain the integration of this type of learning with academics and reduce the chance that the staff will feel overwhelmed and disengage from the process.

Level 3—Benefit to Self and Others

From the leadership's perspective, this level might include how engaging in this type of instruction is going to benefit the school, the teaching staff, and most importantly the students. Level 3 asks one to look beyond themselves, to consider how these attributes can affect the lives of others they encounter. It is essential to think about how one's talents, gifts, and personal beliefs contribute to a productive mankind.

- *Reflect and Connect*—is an instructional technique that asks individuals to reflect on the benefits and challenges of a concept or idea, or reflect on the importance of a concept or idea and support their response with research and evidence. The evidence can be derived from previous professional development or through self-initiated inquiry and research. In this case, reflect and connect could be used to ask staff members to think about how implementing or integrating the 3C's would benefit their students and themselves. It could be a part of training, or it might be "teacher homework" to discuss at a future faculty meeting. This allows teachers time to reflect on the material and information and formulate clear and thoughtful responses to the question.
- *Pilot and assess the effectiveness of the model*—is an essential component of implementation. In a perfect school environment, everyone is on board with models and programs designed to benefit the students and help them find success. However, we live in the real world and realize that there are factions within schools that resist ideas and can be polarizing figures, who embrace their influence in a negative way. A possible circumvention to that problem is to identify those teachers who are open to piloting the model or integrating the learning into their current teaching practices. Have those teachers engage in some practitioner-based research (action research) and later report on the effectiveness of the model with their students. For principals, it might also mean working with the assistant principals, counselors, deans of students, and other support staff, first, and then, integrate the teaching teams later.

Level 4—Action and Embracing Influence

From the administrator's perspective, each level requires some action. However, once the administrators themselves have mastered Levels 1–3, it is time to *embrace the influence* they have as the chief instructional leader and move to take action or motivate others to take action to use the Model of Influence to implement the 3 C's.

This also means that the administrator is empowering their staff members to see themselves as difference makers. As a result, those staff members are hopefully inspired to take action and embrace the influence they

ADVICE FOR SCHOOL LEADERS

have as the chief instructional leaders in their own classrooms. Here are some strategies to consider.

- *Allocating funding for resources*—might include securing high quality professional development, purchasing books, supplies and materials to facilitate in-servicing, book talks, and so forth. It might also mean supporting innovative service-learning projects or other authentic learning experiences, like those illustrated in chapters 4, 5, and 6.
- *Monitoring and assessing the pilot*—are both critical to success. Earlier, we mentioned that a strategy to support level 3—*benefit to self and others*, would be to pilot the model and 3C's in receptive teachers' classrooms. It will be imperative that the administrator supports the teacher's implementation and also monitors and assesses the effectiveness from a school's perspective. Engage the teacher or teaching team in an action research project to collect evidence of the feasibility of the program. Then use teachers' perspectives to inform the implementation process, much in the same way that schools, leaders, and others use performance data to inform the instructional process can be collected as additional evidence.

To avoid feeling like an add-on to the instructional process, we encourage leaders to be strategic in how they implement this process. The goal is to have sustainability of social and emotional development throughout the school's curriculum and for the entire staff to take ownership, see the value in this kind of integration, and ultimately commit to the process.

CREATING PARTNERSHIPS

There are many organizations and businesses willing to partner and invest in education. There are numerous local and global organizations that can be used to facilitate a greater understanding and valuing of compassion, courage, and civility. As mentioned earlier in this chapter, a look at how partnerships are formed might be in order. This might mean that while you are focused on the academic content, you can also build students' social and emotional learning to support their successes in and out of the classroom.

For example, Chicks for Children, Inc. (www.chicksforchildren.org) is an organization that supports both local and global interests in the area of sustainable food, income, and resources. One of the flagship projects from Chicks for Children, Inc., is the Kitale Connection Project. This project has worked with local schools across the country to develop service-learning opportunities for K–6 students. Through this project, young children have engaged in learning activities that focused on all academic content areas and social-emotional learning. As the administrator, building a partnership with this type of organization would allow you to provide teachers with curricular flexibility to teach these attributes more authentically and connect the academic with the social emotional development through service-learning project, for example.

We purport that students will need far more skills than those offered through their academic content. They will need to navigate a world—a future that we help them create. This future is one where they will need to care for others, show compassion to those in need, and take courageous steps to advocate for their needs and the needs of others. As we have suggested throughout this book, there are many more attributes that can and should be integrated into the school's curriculum. The overall outcome is to engage students in authentic learning that integrates their academic and social and emotional development. However, it is not only the families who are responsible for ensuring our students can contribute to the classroom, the community and the world in a significant and profound way. It is also the responsibility of the teacher, the principal, the counselor, and others who will affect that kind of change in the students' lives. While there are many values and attributes that our students will need to be successful, civility, courage, and compassion are at the top of the list.

CONCLUSION

In chapter 1, we sought to make a case for purposeful instruction regarding the concepts of civility, compassion, and courage in our K–12 classrooms. We have asked educators to engage students in lessons, discussions, reflections, and experiences in an effort to foster a valuing of these characteristics. We have cited numerous examples from the media and our current state of the world as we have tried to gently urge the teaching of these concepts. As we come to a close, we quietly hope that this little book will make a small impact on someone's teaching priorities.

Ask any parent, what does he/she want for his/her children? The answer is almost always, a better life, a peaceful, blessed, happy, productive, and satisfying existence in a world that supports the value in every human being. Who among us does not want that for our lives and the lives of those we care about? We purport that one small way to increase the likelihood that this will happen is in how we teach our children to care for each other, to be civil, and to be courageous, even when faced with adversity.

We sincerely believe that, just as the pebble dropped into the lake has far reaching consequences, our book will potentially have an impact on a teacher or two, but more importantly on children's lives. Throughout the writing of this book, we have been cognizant of world events, notably new violence in the Middle East, airplane bombings, heinous crime in ours as well as other communities, road rage, workplace rage, and yes, rage in the schools.

Our belief is that we can't waste any more time setting aside some of our other urgent priorities to devote at the very least, a few minutes per day to the intentional instruction that is required to convey the importance of these three little words—civility, compassion, and courage—to our young people. Our world, and our children's lives depend on it.

We end as we began, with the question posed in chapter 1: what better way to increase one's circle of influence than by seeking to promote civility, compassion, and courage in our children and our future? We once again offer up our colleague Mark Cooper's challenge: "Don't wait for a difference maker—go out and make a difference!

APPENDIX A
LESSON PLAN TEMPLATE

Lesson Plan on: _____

Goal:
Objective:
Focus Level:

Table A1.1

Lesson Content	
Assessments:	
Procedures: Instructional set (brief description) Content • (step by step procedures) • Closing (brief description)	**Materials, Supplies, and Resources:** (bulleted list) **Notes:**

Table A1.2.

Level Extensions: (ideas for applications for next three levels)	
Home and Community Connections: (possible organizations, ideas to do with parents, ways it is demonstrated outside of school)	
Grade Modifications: (ideas for other grades)	

Additional Notes/Reflections/Adaptations:

APPENDIX B

RESOURCES FOR DEVELOPING A POWERPOINT, PREZI, OR BLOG

Prezi

https://prezi.com/support/
https://prezi.com/support/article/steps/get-started-with-prezi/
http://oregonstate.edu/tac/how-to-use/prezi/prezi-teaching-kit
http://prezi.com/explore/staff-picks/
http://blog.prezi.com/

PowerPoint

http://www.brainshark.com/build-it/index (K–12 students would love this! They can use PowerPoint presentations previously created and make them more interesting or engaging.)

http://blog.laptopmag.com/powerpoint-2013-audio-video **How to Add Audio and Video in PowerPoint 2013**

http://www.free-power-point-templates.com/ (Check out the different categories of templates)

http://www.brainybetty.com/MENUPowerPoint5.htm (Check out **Free for PowerPoint** and **Other Free Resources**)

http://www.brainybetty.com/soundsforpowerpoint.htm (FREE music or sounds for PowerPoint)

http://www.brainybetty.com/fonts.htm (Download really cool fonts to jazz up your PowerPoint)

http://www.brainybetty.com/flashtitleslides.htm (Flash animations for PowerPoint--Note the introductory information)
http://www.watchknowlearn.org/
http://www.grsites.com/archive/sounds/category/18/?offset=0

Blogs

news@edublogs.org (***edublogs*** is an online newsletter with endless FREE tech tips and tools)
http://us1.campaign-archive1.com/?u=53a1e972a043d1264ed082a5b&id=726013b260&e=59a257e2c4
Check out ***What is a blog?*** and ***Learning to Teach Online***.